T0046278

The Roof of
the Whale Poems

WISCONSIN POETRY SERIES

Sean Bishop and Jesse Lee Kercheval, *series editors*
Ronald Wallace, *founding series editor*

The Roof of
the Whale Poems

Juan Calzadilla

Translated by Katherine M. Hedeen *and* Olivia Lott

THE UNIVERSITY OF WISCONSIN PRESS

Publication of this book has been made possible, in part, through support from the Brittingham Trust.

The University of Wisconsin Press
728 State Street, Suite 443
Madison, Wisconsin 53706
uwpress.wisc.edu

Gray's Inn House, 127 Clerkenwell Road
London EC1R 5DB, United Kingdom
eurospanbookstore.com

Originally published under the titles *Dictado por la jauría* (1962), *Malos modales* (1965), and *Las contradicciones sobrenaturales* (1967) by Juan Calzadilla, copyright © Ediciones del Techo de la Ballena, Caracas
Translation copyright © 2023 by Katherine M. Hedeen and Olivia Lott
All rights reserved. Except in the case of brief quotations embedded in critical articles and reviews, no part of this publication may be reproduced, stored in a retrieval system, transmitted in any format or by any means—digital, electronic, mechanical, photocopying, recording, or otherwise—or conveyed via the Internet or a website without written permission of the University of Wisconsin Press. Rights inquiries should be directed to rights@uwpress.wisc.edu.

Printed in the United States of America
This book may be available in a digital edition.

Library of Congress Cataloging-in-Publication Data
Names: Calzadilla, Juan, author. | Calzadilla, Juan. Dictado por la jauría. English | Calzadilla, Juan. Malos modales. English | Calzadilla, Juan. Contradicciones sobrenaturales. English | Hedeen, Katherine M., translator. | Lott, Olivia, translator.
Title: The Roof of the Whale poems / Juan Calzadilla ; translated by Katherine M. Hedeen and Olivia Lott.
Other titles: Wisconsin poetry series.
Description: Madison, Wisconsin : The University of Wisconsin Press, 2023. | Series: Wisconsin poetry series | Originally published under the titles Dictado por la jauría (1962), Malos modales (1965), and Las contradicciones sobrenaturales (1967) by Juan Calzadilla, copyright © Ediciones del Techo de la Ballena, Caracas.
Identifiers: LCCN 2023019888 | ISBN 9780299346645 (paperback)
Subjects: LCGFT: Poetry.
Classification: LCC PQ8550.13.A37 R66 2023 | DDC 861/.64—dc23/eng/20230719
LC record available at https://lccn.loc.gov/2023019888

Contents

Las contradicciones sobrenaturales / The Supernatural Contradictions (1967)

Foreword

Víctor Rodríguez Núñez

We should celebrate with great fanfare that the superb poetry of Juan Calzadilla has begun to be recognized beyond the Spanish language. Even more so, he has been brought into English at the hands of Katherine M. Hedeen and Olivia Lott, a duo of brilliant translators. As if that weren't enough, this edition has reached the world awarded by the notable poet and translator Forrest Gander. And, finally, its pages bring together the three collections of poems published by the Venezuelan author during those foundational days of El Techo de la Ballena (The Roof of the Whale). For the book you hold in your hands, the old saying that the stars have aligned has never been more accurate.

Juan Calzadilla is the paradigm of a complete artist. His singular writing, encompassing poetry, narrative, essays, journalism, translation, and editing, has been recognized in Venezuela with the 2017 National Prize in Literature. He is also a visual artist, a curator, and a no less exceptional art critic, which earned him the 1996 National Prize in the Visual Arts. But out of all his multiple and consummate vocations, distinct focal points for his immeasurable creative energy, the most fundamental is poetry. His books, which have appeared in Argentina, Brazil, Colombia, Cuba, and Spain, place him among the most esteemed and influential poets of the Spanish language.

El Techo de la Ballena (1961–69) is the group that, in Venezuela, managed to fuse the political avant-garde and the aesthetic avant-garde with the greatest consequence, and to earn a reputation beyond the country's borders. By appropriating the postulates and modes of action of the early twentieth-century European avant-gardes, particularly those with a Marxist approach, these intellectuals confronted the established powers in the

social and cultural spheres. Calzadilla was one of its most active members and the one who has most faithfully sustained his theory and practice to this day. In his case, he has attempted something much more than *épater les bourgeois*: to take the discourse of the ruling class by storm and remove them from power.

The books gathered here have forged radical new paths for poetry in the Spanish language by profoundly denouncing the foundational dehumanization of modernity—deformed and dependent, in the case of Venezuela, being a country that is a casualty of colonialism. Within this critique, the poems also appropriate surrealist language—as is characteristic of a poet with a decolonizing will. Faced with the city as a metonym for capitalist society, Calzadilla's speaker resorts to the negation of the negation, or, in other words, to dialectical identification. We are before an ecological poetry by omission—its devastating representation of the artificial world is, ultimately, an affirmation of the natural world.

I celebrate Calzadilla's commitment to dialogic poetry, which abandons romantic solipsism and the illusory objectivity of realism. With intellectual clairvoyance, his work seeks the dissolution of the unitary, coherent, autonomous subject that is at the root of modern-day ravaging and devastation. Along with fundamentally attacking bourgeois individualism, this poetry is clearly offered up as a representation of reality, not as reality itself. Thus, it calls for a participative, active reader: a coauthor of the work, if you will. It is my great hope that this project, radical to its core but not normative or dogmatic—and respectful of different positions—will resonate with English-language poets and readers just as it has with so many from the Spanish-speaking world.

Introduction

The Magma Must Return

Katherine M. Hedeen and Olivia Lott

In 1961, in Caracas, Venezuela, Juan Calzadilla cofounded the radical arts collective El Techo de la Ballena (The Roof of the Whale). Active from 1961 to 1969, the group brought together young poets, visual artists, and essayists united in the task of confronting the system: shaking Venezuelan social order and scandalizing established artistic values. The balleneros (or "whalers") were energized by the 1959 triumph of the Cuban Revolution and the anti-imperialist revolutionary fervor that swept Latin America in the 1960s. In the wake of the African liberation movements of the 1950s, the Cuban model provided hope that large-scale social transformation was not only possible but inevitable. In turn, the continent's artists and thinkers were called to action: to make the revolution in the cultural sphere by any means necessary. The avant-garde returned, and new forms of art proliferated, transforming art, literature, and film into actual weapons for revolutionary struggle. Borders of nation, language, and genre were defied, as artists sought to empower the public as socially conscious agents.[1]

By the early 1960s in Caracas, Venezuela was deep into the implementation of a developmentalist agenda that ultimately served imperialist powers and the nation's ruling class. The dictatorship of Marcos Pérez Jiménez had been overthrown in 1958, but his New National Ideal (1948–58) mostly remained intact under new president Rómulo Betancourt. The ultranationalist program funneled the country's oil revenues into modernist architecture and urban planning, linked to the promise of full modernity for all. The official slogan pledged "the rational transformation of the physical environment and the moral, intellectual, and material improvement of

the country's inhabitants." In practice, the state projected a shiny image of progress, while obscuring a reality of worsening socioeconomic inequity, repression, and police violence. Termed "deformed" or "lopsided" modernity, there was effectively one Caracas for the rich, another for everyone else—and their separation was militantly enforced.[2]

The Roof of the Whale sought to mobilize the avant-garde to raise consciousness to the realities of uneven modernity in Caracas and thus participate in the continental revolutionary undertaking. Members penned manifestos (often reworking surrealist techniques), staged Dadaesque public interventions, held polemical art exhibitions, and published poetry and essays under their own editorial label. Rejecting the mass-marketed image of progress, the whalers resolved to investigate trash and capitalist dehumanization, building art from the literal and metaphoric by-products. In contrast to the rigid dividing lines of the modernizing agenda, the group routinely evoked the metaphor of magma, whose boundless fluidity served as a theoretical axis for new social and aesthetic possibilities. The prominent Latin American cultural critic Ángel Rama famously labeled these practices "art terrorism" and called the collective an "urban guerrilla." Rama highlights specific strategies of audience ambush and the generation of new, collective art forms "capable of reaching vulnerable points in the structure of domination."[3]

Calzadilla (b. 1931 in Altagracia de Orituco, Venezuela) was a major participant in the collective. He contributed paintings, coauthored manifestos, and published three poetry collections: *Dictado por la jauría* (*Dictated by the Pack*, 1962), *Malos modales* (*Bad Manners*, 1965), and *Las contradicciones sobrenaturales* (*The Supernatural Contradictions*, 1967). Our edition, *The Roof of the Whale Poems*, includes full translations of each of these collections, marking the first time that these texts have been gathered together, in English or Spanish. The writings of Calzadilla, known as the "poet of Caracas," are driven by the city—the contamination, dehumanization, and alienation it spawns—and surrealist techniques: chaotic enumeration, stream of consciousness, radical juxtaposition. A similar aesthetics guides his visual arts, which draw heavily on automated drawing and sequential repetition. His most famous paintings are populated by wandering, contorting figures arranged in cinematographic strips.[4]

Across these *Roof of the Whale Poems*, Calzadilla illuminates an urban space where the spectacle of Venezuela's modernity displays its cracks: its

gardens overflow with pus, luxury spas are flooded with lava, blood trickles down beneath the floorboards. The urban center appears as a "magisterial concrete jungle" that "digests all its victims." It collapses in on the poetic subject, who finds "no exit sites" because "all the doors are mysteriously shut." The city-turned-cage ossifies his eyelids, pounds jackknives into his cranium, sics vultures on his bowels. It turns him into an insect, a virus, a cannibal, a poetic subject-made-abject. In the end, his fully evolved form is as a prisoner who must perform his crimes for the powerbrokers and subject himself to torture. A chain twists around his neck, someone points a dagger at the inside of his eye, a hearing leads to an emergency surgery to amputate his "sick side."

Trapped in this environment, the speaker rules out the possibility of salvation by divine means: guards dig into his forehead "like holy water"; crucifixion paintings appear in urinals whose walls are "gallows-thick"; the speaker confesses to selling his angel, killing it "with a clumsy knife un-washed." But the "illogicality" of capitalist modernity also proves wholly incapable of resurrecting a humane society. In "waiting for salvation," the business sector celebrates a "surplus of zeros," an "incredible excess of zeros," and its lucrative strategies: the conversion of train tickets into death certificates and the production of "exaggeratedly large" cadavers. Elsewhere Venezuela's modern capitalism is depicted as a card game, a roll of the dice, a rigged game of Russian roulette. Eventually, the city takes the speaker over, seizes his movements, while repressing screams under his skin. Both inmate and executioner, he orders the ousting of his organs; he instructs his brain to be "emptied like an eye over a rock."

It is through these evolutions—eerie, disturbing, visceral—that Calza-dilla's poems become a counterpoint to the New National Ideal's promise of modernity for all and the Betancourt administration's claim to superior democratic governance. The poems provide the tools to the reader to un-mask dominant ideology and the grand narrative of progress via superficial transformation. In other words, within the unreal of Calzadilla's urban jungle lies the possibility of glimpsing the real: capitalist modernity as a facade for growing the wealth and criminal immunity of the rich and pow-erful, while leaving everyone else worse off.

Birthed in the crises and awakenings of the 1960s, these poems increas-ingly speak to the social inequity, daily death, and naturalized violence that we live through today. Calzadilla's chronicling of the flimsiness of democracy

(his speaker-turned-prisoner never knows what he has been charged for) alongside the violence of modern labor (the "suicide briefcase," the suffocation of suits, the desk meant to carry under your arm as a "bearable grave") may read as if it was already written for us.

Translating Calzadilla's poetry can be likened to "a descent of jackknives along [the] cranium." Our heads abuzz with "larval hatcheries," with "the darkzone of eyelids," with "humid violaceous fungus." Here there are no guardrails, no possibility of detachment from the disturbing reality at hand. Jagged, unpredictable, generative of a chaotic poetic space: these same vertiginous movements guide our English. We refuse to hide the "bullet-shattered glass," to silence the "hymns in the sewer ablution," and instead highlight the violence and gore that drive the speaker. We defy the "general order." Even formally, we follow Calzadilla's lead, his spirit of nonconformity. We have adopted his disregard for rules of punctuation, so prominent in *Dictated by the Pack*, across all three books. We honor the ununiform employment of capital letters and defamiliarizing syntax throughout; we respect section titles, which produce both fusions and fissures within each collection. Calzadilla's dialogic impulse is essential to the broader Roof of the Whale project and it is at the center of our translational poetics. We draw you in.

Calzadilla and The Roof of the Whale sought to empower a specific public at a specific time, creating art that could disrupt the mythos of progress of their era. To translate Calzadilla's work during our own moment of crisis—of the COVID-19 pandemic, climate collapse, social unrest, and the necropolitics of late-stage capitalism—is, in some way, to unleash the whalers' 1960s consciousness-raising project on a new 2020s readership: the return of the magma, our most ambitious goal. Reader: "It is the day of your departure take everything you need . . ." We leave the rest up to you.

Notes

1. For more on the 1960s in Latin America, we especially recommend Claudia Gilman, *Entre la pluma y el fusil: Debates y dilemas del escritor revolucionario en América Latina* (Buenos Aires: Siglo XXI, 2013); Diana Sorensen *A Turbulent Decade Remembered: Scenes from the Latin American Sixties* (Stanford: Stanford University Press, 2007).

2. For more on midcentury modernization in Venezuela, see Lisa Blackmore, *Spectacular Modernity: Dictatorship, Space, and Visuality in Venezuela, 1948–1958* (Pittsburgh: University of Pittsburgh Press, 2017); Fernando Coronil, *The Magical State: Nature, Money, and Modernity in Venezuela* (Chicago: University of Chicago Press, 1997). The slogan of the New National Ideal may be found in *Venezuela bajo el Nuevo Ideal Nacional* (Caracas: Imprenta Nacional, 1956).

3. Rama's essay serves as the prologue to *Antología de "El Techo de la Ballena,"* ed. Ángel Rama (Caracas: Fundarte, 1987). For more on El Techo de la Ballena, we recommend María C. Gaztambide, *El Techo de la Ballena: Retro-Modernity in Venezuela* (University of Florida Press, 2019); Olivia Lott, "In (Dis)Use of Reason: Abjection Poetics and Macrocephalic Modernity in El Techo de la Ballena," *Revista Hispánica Moderna* 75, no. 1 (2022): 22–39; Sean Nesselrode Moncada, "The Painting Devoured: El Techo de la Ballena and the Destruction of Venezuelan Informalism," in *New Geographies of Abstract Art in Postwar Latin America*, ed. Mariola V. Álvarez and Ana M. Franco (New York: Routledge, 2018), 41–65.

4. For more on Calzadilla, see Paul W. Borgeson Jr., "Juan Calzadilla y el surrealismo en la poesía venezolana del '58," *Revista Iberoamericana* 60, nos. 166–67 (1994): 513–22; Arturo Gutiérrez Plaza, "Apuntes para una lectura de(sde) la ciudad y lo urbano de(sde) la poesía venezolana," *Hispamérica* 35, no. 150 (2006): 3–16.

Dictado por la jauría
Dictated by the Pack
(1962)

DICTADO POR LA JAURÍA

DICTATED BY THE PACK

vivo a diario   puesto que no debo arriesgarme
mido bien con mis pasos la calle y cuento con manos salobres de sudor
cada minuto en que estuve a punto de morir
a los árboles deseo encontrar en sus sitios de antes
así soy tengo miedo amo la lluvia cuídome de todo como buen
empresario que sabe administrar sus años
cuídame del sol mi cabeza opuesta al sueño
vivo a diario   leo la prensa me subo a los titulares como sabandija
trepada al cráneo de un turista
me abro paso entre la multitud ondeando diariamente
bestia holgazana cierro los ojos y digo túnel carnívoro sin omitir sílaba
me saludan las bocinas y digo cueva de occiso es tu boca preparada
para los funerales
me introduzco en los edificios sin salida un día cualquiera
rodéame magistral selva de concreto en ese instante
en que una puerta se abre para cerrar otra
redúzcome   pierdo peso y altura y me he dicho
desciende juan del último piso
y decido no lanzarme dándome postín que mueve a risa en estos tiempos
pues vivir en ellos es enorme empresa
y río de primero sin llegar a ser el último
y rio de último siendo el primero
rio de miedo-pánico y de hambre canina cuando la ciudad hace
la digestión de todas sus víctimas
        que sueñan sin poder dormir
y que duermen sin poder soñar
y como cerviz de toro inexperto que cuelga en los mataderos
mi ojo grosero siempre dispuesto a vaciarse como vaso de vino
yo metódico hombre tedioso rey en su casa pido clemencia pido
    clemencia

i live day by day   since i better not take any chances
i measure the street with my stride and with my hands salty with sweat
i count each minute when i was about to die
i want to see the trees in the same place as before
that's me i'm scared i love the rain i take care of myself like a good
manager who knows how to supervise his years
my head against sleep protects me from the sun
i live day by day   read the papers climb the headlines like a bug
up a tourist's skull
i make my way through the crowd's daily rippling
lazy beast i close my eyes and say carnivorous tunnel i don't miss a syllable
car horns greet me and i say murder-victim cave is your mouth prepared
for funerals
any given day i go into buildings with no way out
magisterial concrete jungle surrounds me then
when a door opens to close another
i am marked down   lose weight and height and i've told myself
juan come down from the top floor
and i decide not to jump show-off laughable in these times
since living through them is an enormous venture
and i laugh first but won't be the last
and i laugh last being the first
i laugh out of fearpanic and canine hunger when the city
digests all its victims
          dreaming but unable to sleep
and sleeping but unable to dream
and like an inexpert bull nape hanging in the slaughterhouse
my impolite gaze always willing to empty like a wine glass
me methodic man tedious king in his home i ask for mercy i ask for
    mercy

funcionario que celebra un ritual   funcionario que celebra un ritual
alrededor de su ombligo que trota hasta más no poder
y se odia a sí mismo cada mañana bajo el sol de la avenida
        fumando escupiendo estornudando
disertando bajo un agua de ángeles que gorjea en los ascensores
pues digo yo qué otra cosa puedo hacer sino ser yo mismo
gritando con todos mis ladridos negándome vanagloriándome
de mis acciones curvado por el peso de las urnas sobre una gota
de saliva para revivir una hazaña perdida
haciendo eses por la calle más viejo que de costumbre
buen hablador que guarda silencio en público eso sí
más que todo convertido en ave de rapiña
orinando diciéndome cada mañana el tiempo es oro
el tiempo no es una memoria el tiempo es una pared donde el ciego
escribe sin comprender
mirando los murciélagos en mi habitación
gritan tan alto como yo me ahogan en mi propio grito
sienten vergüenza de mí
debo tener sin embargo una voz probablemente una bella voz
me he dicho a mí mismo mas quién me ha de oír si lo que hago
es chillar aquí abajo
ebrio de felicidad alguna vez me recuerdo tamborileando sobre la lluvia
con dedos mojados en cerveza
extraño tam tam emerge en domingo desde mi oficina
cuento hasta diez   dónde me he de ocultar esta vez
todas las puertas están misteriosamente selladas
dónde hacer aquello   arrójaseme de todas partes
arrójaseme del sueño arrójaseme de mí mismo
y el brillo de un año nuevo me encandila de repente
        sol agrietado que irrumpe a través de los vidrios del año nuevo
    me inundo   me inundo
hay que reconocerlo no estoy hecho para dirigir la multitud

a civil servant celebrates a ritual   a civil servant celebrates a ritual
around his belly button on the go until he can't go on
hates himself each morning under the avenue sun
        smoking spitting sneezing
speaks at length under an angel water gurgling in the elevators
and i just say what else can i do but be myself
shouting with all my barks refusing bragging
about my actions bent by the weight of ballot boxes over a drop
of spit to relive a feat lost
zigzagging down the street older than normal
motormouth shuts up in public it's true
more than anything turned into a bird of prey
pissing each morning telling me time is money
time is not a memory time is a wall where the blind
write but don't understand
watching the bats in my room
screech as loud as me they drown me in my own scream
they are ashamed of me
though i must have a voice probably a beautiful voice
i've told myself but who's going to hear me if all i do
is shriek deep down
drunk on happiness i remember one time drumming on the rain
my fingers dripped with beer
on sunday a strange boom ba boom coming from my office
i count to ten   where do i hide this time
all the doors are mysteriously shut
where to go   throw me down from everywhere
throw me down from dream throw me down from me
and a new year beam suddenly dazes me
        sun cracked bursts through new year windows
    i am flooded   i am flooded
it's time to face it i wasn't made to lead the crowd

y algo espeso como pulpa de café se adhiere a mis ojos
pega sus presentimientos a mi piel   agota mi enorme paciencia
cómo desprenderme de todo esto si no puedo mudar de piel
otra vez grito se me ha encerrado aquí estoy sentado como
        jonás sobre un barril de pólvora
se me ordena salir ya es tarde estoy atado al poste

and something thick like coffee pulp gets stuck in my eyes
sticks its premonitions to my skin   wears out my great patience
how to get it all off if i cannot shed my skin
i scream again i am trapped in here i am sitting like
        jonah on a barrel of gunpowder
they're making me leave it's getting late i am tied to the pole

escorpión   los experimentos se muestran insaciables repiten
un naipe donde antes había un clavel unen dos puntos separados
por el largo de un cadáver
extendiendo esa capa de asfalto verde que la tierra llega a conocer
sólo cuando se la ha chupado inmediatamente
embozados cadáveres de tinta que crepitan en todas las
páginas que envejecen como esos restos de perro en la acera
que nadie acoge que no encuentran un sitio de reposo y que cansados
de esperar en los cuadros de los museos
vuelven como por instinto sus mandíbulas hacia el oscuro
visitante que entonces deberá huir
como si fuese tu piel de combatiente y no el cuadro famoso
lo que pegas a la pared un minuto antes de volver y oyeras
no en la plaza pública sino en tu propio cuarto desatarse la jauría
mientras tú permaneces sentado ahí sin moverte y actuaras
como el perro sin dueño cuyos ladridos te enseñan a comportarte
mas siendo como el alacrán en el pico del cuervo

scorpion   the experiments seem voracious having seconds
of a playing card where once there was a carnation they join two separate
    points
along the length of a corpse
stretching the layer of green asphalt the earth gets to know it better
only when it has sucked it down straightaway
muffled ink corpses crackle on every
page they age like those dog remains on the sidewalk
nobody takes them in no resting place they are tired
of waiting in museum paintings
out of instinct their jaws return to the dark
visitor who should run away then
as if it were your combatant skin and not the famed painting
you hang on the wall a minute before showing up and you heard
the pack letting loose not out in public but in your own room
while you just sit there motionless and you pretended
to be a stray dog whose barking tells you what to do
but like the scorpion on a crow's beak

vecindad del buitre   esta sustracción espantosa que gritando en los residuos de víscera que lleva cada cuervo acomete por última vez mi lado izquierdo picotea mi vientre mantiene con sus gritos escandalizado a todo un vecindario nada más que a esa comunidad bien informada de todo que finalmente se pone de parte del buitre para irrumpir también en mis vísceras con sus lamentos de perro

vulture neighborhood   this frightening subtraction crying out in the visceral residues carried by each crow attacks my left side for the last time pecks at my belly with its cries keeps the whole neighborhood in an uproar nothing more than this well-informed community that finally takes the vulture's side and barges into my viscera as well with its dog moans

esperando salvación   los números ceros atraviesan las paredes
de los cráneos limpios de conciencia   se internan por el ojo de los
funcionarios a quienes atormenta la manía de contar
que padecen en silencio sus miopías con sus trajes limpios
mientras sueñan despiadadamente en sus jaulas comunes
sin olvidar sus desvelos de padres múltiples ni su avidez
de contar todo lo que está al alcance de sus manos
agachándose bajo una orden cuando por distracción
algún número solitario cae al suelo para recogerlo y extenderlo
de nuevo sobre la mesa igual que a un hueso de ballena que necesita
de una exacta comprobación
allí mismo comienzan a sobrar ceros cifras humillantes que enloquecen
al encargado de poner fuego a los billetes de banco
sucios ajados billetes sin dueño que
derrite la carnicería de esta llama infamante
     y ya no hay ceniza en los dientes sino boletos de tren
que después de todo se transforman en partidas de defunción
     se ha producido un excedente increíble de ceros hacia todos
lados los funcionarios no saben qué hacer
con sus esqueletos retorcidos como hierro viejo bajo tormentas de papel
     sus esqueletos aguardando salvación
sus esqueletos demasiado grandes donde ya no caben
ni qué hacer con su desmedida sed de lucro y su celo colmado
de hojas amarillas que sobrepasan el tamaño de todas sus desdichas

sus cadáveres exageradamente grandes

waiting for salvation   the number zeros crisscross the walls
of the skulls with a clear conscious   pierce the eyes
of civil servants tormented by the mania of counting
suffering their nearsightedness in silence with their clean suits
while heartlessly dreaming in common cages
they don't forget their insomnias of multiple fathers or their eagerness
for counting everything close at hand
crouched beneath an order when out of distraction
some solitary number falls to the floor to be picked up and placed
once more on the table just like a whale bone needing
an exact verification
right then appears a surplus of zeros humiliating amounts they drive
the one in charge of lighting the bank bills on fire mad
dirty crumpled ownerless bills
melt the meat market of this shameful flame
      and instead of ash in their teeth there are train tickets
now transformed to death certificates
        an incredible excess of zeros everywhere has
come about the civil servants don't know what to do
with their skeletons twisted like old iron beneath paper storms
        their skeletons awaiting salvation
their skeletons so large they no longer fit
or what to do about their boundless thirst for profit and overflowing zeal
for yellow leaves surpassing the size of all their misfortune

their cadavers exaggeratedly large

gracias al barniz   los cuadros viven de las frases al oído de los buenos modales de los motivos de la adoración de los reyes y la esclerosis del millonario de un paisaje de selva urbana de un cuarto detestable de barrio latino para alcoba refinada o sencillamente de los desnudos de mujer originariamente tendidos para la venta pública miles de cuadros comienzan a vivir cuando se descorre la cortina alargando la mano bajo un martillo y un conteo de grandes cifras hasta tres que rueda por las escaleras precediendo a esos desastres marítimos que arruinan una casa de buena familia y se oyen ruidos de pasos en el salón y ladridos de perros   nada tiene de extraño que el cuadro experimente uno de esos bruscos cambios de escena de pronto descubrimos que nada existe en la mirada el cuadro se ha vaciado como un ojo bajo una impostura   la memoria siente nostalgia tiene hambre necesita de ganchos al igual que la ropa o la fotografía y la obra de arte a su vez necesita de la pistola del suicida y la buena conducta y las lecciones de geografía dictadas cerca del fuego junto al perro de raza etcétera   por todas partes el mundo se despelleja se desgaja han aumentado el número de bedeles de goya se rumia óleo sagrado servido en marcos nuevos rostros sin envejecer durante trescientos años no eran ayer más que jovencitas de hoy día gracias al barniz hemos cambiado sólo de aspecto pero el amor lleva el mismo traje hemos cambiado las costumbres la esperanza está perdida galanes rejuvenecidos por una fiesta perpetua gracias al barniz conservan los modales de la época el renacimiento y todo lo que viene antes porque gracias al barniz la pintura muda de dueño se cobra sus ruinas se cierra lo que en adelante necesitará una llave maestra para descifrar el ojo de la cerradura cediendo mostrándonos flores carnales y flores auténticas toda clase de trajes el cuerno de caza el retrato del emperador la sombra espesa del seno de una maja turbada por los gusanos que descienden a su sexo de terciopelo ebrio como si el ayer fuera siempre una rosa pura

thanks to the varnish   the paintings live off whispered phrases good manners motives adoration kings and millionaire sclerosis off an urban jungle landscape a detestable room in the latin quarter as a refined chamber or simply off the female nudes originally hung for sale to the public thousands of paintings begin to live when the curtain is drawn back lengthening the hand beneath a hammer and a counting of great amounts up to three rolling down the stairs preceding the maritime disasters that ruin the home of a good family and you hear the sound of steps in the hall and dogs barking   it is not strange at all that the painting experiences one of those abrupt changes of scene suddenly we discover nothing exists in the gaze the painting is emptied like an eye beneath an imposture   memory feels nostalgia is hungry needs hangers like clothes or photos and a work of art needs a suicide gun and good behavior and geography lessons dictated by the fire next to a pure-bred dog etcetera   everywhere the world is skinned splits off the number of goya custodians has gone up sacred oil is ruminated served in new frames faces unaged for three hundred years yesterday they were nothing more than young girls from the present day thanks to the varnish we've only changed our look but love wears the same suit we've changed our customs hope is lost courtiers rejuvenated by a perpetual party thanks to the varnish the manners of the era the renaissance and everything before are conserved because thanks to the varnish owner's silent painting claims its ruins closed what from now on will need a master key to decode the key hole ceding showing us carnal flowers and authentic flowers every kind of suit the hunting horn the emperor's portrait the heavy shadow of the breast of a maja worried about the worms descending toward her velvety drunk sex as if the past were always a pure rose

mingitorio   estos muros con espesor de lava y mar cuya existencia
suda horriblemente no se están quietos ni un minuto más
bucean con un ojo consternado que silba en el interior de las lámparas
de enfermería basculando en los torrentes de sangre que ascienden
hasta el techo en el tóxico de los sismos y en las corrientes
de las aves migratorias
engastados bajo marcas de almohadas
semejantes a la esponja marina

     entre sueños de epilépticos con su sed de discordias y sus sillas
de ruedas hechas para el amor de los palúdicos cuyos nombres
borrados por la lluvia ya olvidaron sus primeras amantes
en fin estos muros de fiesta propicios para toda confesión
estos muros que se enroscan mudando de corteza como una serpiente
muros con piel de lava y espesor de cadalso que muestran en sus grietas
esos cuadros de crucifixión que hacen delirar a las vértebras

estos muros en desuso

urinal   these walls thick with lava and sea whose being
sweats uncontrollably cannot stand still a minute longer
they dive with a distraught eye whistling inside the infirmary
lamps swinging on bloodstreams that rise
up to the roof in the earthquake toxin and in the currents
of migratory birds
mounted under pillow tides
just like sea sponges
    in dreams of epileptics with their thirst for discord and their wheel
chairs made for malarial lovers whose names
erased by rain have already forgotten their first lovers
in brief these celebratory walls just right for all confessions
these walls coil up shedding cortex like a snake
walls lava-skinned and gallows-thick displaying in between their cracks
the crucifixion paintings that make vertebrates delirious

these walls in disuse

una sala de juego   los escritorios son colocados en una superficie pulida especie de llanura desolada frente a la cual si se estableciera rápidamente una comparación las pirámides parecerían simples burbujas de sol   así se ha intentado llenar el mundo de objetos que hacen imposible la respiración familiar de los muros que rebosan materialmente el marco acordado a la mirada   a despecho del orden que reina se ha impedido nuestra entrada al mundo se la ha sellado increíblemente con toda suerte de obstáculos y maquinaria pesada ya se trate de sillas rotuladoras cañones o pianos de cola el mundo se superpuebla se llena de ruidos se lo ha convertido astutamente en una sala de juego

a cardroom   the desks are placed on a polished surface a kind of desolate plain in front of which if a comparison could be quickly established the pyramids would seem simple sun bubbles   this is how it's been attempted to fill the world with objects that make the familiar breathing of walls impossible that materially overflow the framework agreed upon by sight   out of spite for the reigning order our entrance into the world has been blocked unbelievably it's been sealed with all kinds of obstacles and heavy machinery including but not limited to chairs felt-tip pens cannons or grand pianos the world becomes overpopulated filled with noises has cleverly turned into a cardroom

me reconozco   me reconozco en mi infancia en mi madurez
en mi muerte en los términos de mi oficio de espectador a quien el muro
endurece para siempre
me reconozco en mi córnea de salamandra furiosa
me reconozco en la selva urbana que me propone una máscara
para dar los buenos días desde una claraboya demasiado alta
me reconozco en la oscuridad donde dejo de verme y en medio
de mi alegría cifrada por los despojos de miseria que apuñala mi ojo
      me reconozco en el banco de cárcel negra y en la materia que
osifica mis párpados y diluye mi cráneo nuevo
            que no es sino ese fortalecimiento de sábanas
que busca un punto de apoyo en mi rótula
la súbita aparición del pus que insemina los bellos jardines
de un dispensario nocturno
mis párpados sin venganza mis párpados sin origen mis párpados
sin orificios de salida para cantar para verter loas en témpanos
de dicha interna mis párpados cerrados siempre para ver el lado oscuro
de la carne
a modo de gusanos que pudren mis odios
me reconozco
me reconozco en mi infancia en mi madurez en mi muerte

i see me   i see me in my childhood in my adulthood
in my death in the terms of my profession as a spectator hardened
by the wall for always
i see me in my furious salamander cornea
i see me in the urban jungle it suggests a mask
to say good morning from an impossibly high skylight
i see me in the darkness where i no longer see me and in the midmost
of my happiness coded by the spoils of misery it stabs me in the eye
        i see me on the bench of a dark prison and in the matter
ossifying my eyelids and diluting my new cranium
            which is nothing more than this sheet strengthening
in search of a support point in my kneecap
the sudden appearance of pus inseminating the beautiful gardens
of a nighttime dispensary
my eyelids no vengeance my eyelids no origin my eyelids
no exit sites to sing to spill praises in ice floes
of internal fortune my eyelids closed always to see the dark side
of flesh
like worms rotting my hatreds
i see me
i see me in my childhood in my adulthood in my death

los métodos necesarios   las costumbres han hecho de mí
un ser abominable
impaciente aguardo todo el día como un funcionario
privado del sueño a quien se le obliga a permanecer amarrado
eternamente a su silla
el empresario ha cubierto el cielo con un paraguas ha hecho del mundo
un lugar apto para un crimen ha reducido increíblemente a los
hombres al tamaño de una bala
             más valdría hacer algo te digo
dispararlos remover los escombros para buscar una salida olvidar todo
propósito inconcebible y constituir la felicidad a cualquier precio
y del modo más inmediato con tablas de toda ley de todo naufragio
de toda ferocidad para tener sobre qué morir el día venidero
y adaptar esa muerte a un fin necesario hecho a su propia medida
reducir la dicha a términos humanos como mueble
que entra por casa de pobre
              y crearla en nombre de todos
por todos los medios que estén a la vista por los medios lícitos
e ilícitos por medio del bien y por medio del mal
utilizando todos los métodos los métodos pacíficos y los métodos bélicos
por los métodos más violentos incluyendo el suicidio

the necessary methods   habits have made me
an abominable being
impatiently i wait the whole day like a sleep-deprived
civil servant obliged to stay stuck
eternally to his chair
the manager has covered the sky with an umbrella has made the world
a suitable place for crime incredibly has reduced
people to the size of a bullet
              i'm telling you it would be better to do something
shoot them dig around the debris in search of a way out forget every
inconceivable proposal and constitute happiness at any cost
and in the most immediate way with tables for every law every shipwreck
every ferocity to have something to die on the coming day
and adapt that death to a necessary end made to measure
reduce good fortune to human terms like furnishings
in a poor man's house
              and create in the name of all
by all the means in sight by both licit and illicit
means by good means and bad means
using all the methods peaceful methods and bellicose methods
by the most violent methods including suicide

he sido otro   diariamente soy empujado a ser otro
y el papel me va bien
los modales de reptil con que cubro las apariencias abruman la soledad
de mis trajes desmedidos arruinan el efecto de mis máscaras
los péndulos estas nodrizas insaciables azuzan sus jaurías
me sacan de mis grandes investigaciones me observan
desde otra realidad que hace imposible mi sueño
desde las cribas de enormes baúles marinos
y en el fondo de las habitaciones baldadas de helechos
vuelven mi vida un curso de río donde se baña un leproso
me miran con ojos de flecha desgastada cuyo brillo
yo no sabría olvidar
me he transformado en otro
y el papel me va bien
                    ¿y los paisajes?
veo hacia dentro mapas de carne con mis párpados
de murciélago ablandados sobre un poste
veo siembras de papel en los osarios
he vuelto de revés mi traje para cubrir las apariencias
llevo una máscara
he sido otro

he sustituido mi derecho a la felicidad por la experiencia del crimen
atribuyéndome esa falta de lógica capaz de reactivar en la sonrisa de un
idiota las causas recónditas de un asesinato

i have been another   i am pushed to be another daily
and the role is going pretty well
the reptile manners i cover up appearances with crush the solitude
of my poor-fitting suits pendulums ruin the effect of my masks
these insatiable wet nurses sic their packs
remove me from my great investigations observe me
from another reality that makes sleep impossible
from the sieves of enormous marine trunks
and in the far end of rooms tiled with ferns
they make my life a river's course where a leper bathes
they look at me with the eyes of a frayed arrow whose brilliance
i would not know how to forget
i have been turned into another
and the role is going pretty well
                            what about the landscapes?
i see inside flesh maps with my bat eyelids
softened over a pole
i see sown fields of paper in the ossuaries
i have turned my suit inside out to cover up appearances
i wear a mask
i have been another

i have substituted my right to happiness for the experience of the crime
attributing to myself this illogicality capable of reactivating the hidden
causes of a murder in the smile of an idiot

golpeando el abismo   entre mi espíritu y yo están mis trajes
se levantan mis actos los muros de espesor de luciola
que admito desconocer como al tejido violento de los cromosomas
los abismos blandos que se incrustan a mi cuerpo
hecho de una materia de lava cosmogónica y nervio
de convulsión doméstica
de tumor amistoso con forma de cráter medicinal
una sustancia hecha de corpúsculos de existencia diaria
provistos del tiempo necesario para cada pulsación
y cada uno de los cuales es al mismo tiempo un átomo
un ángel una obra de arte un ser humano
un dios de espesa crin solar
diariamente adquiero conciencia de ese equilibro
de arco peligrosamente tendido
a que me condena un pensamiento a punto de dispararse

hitting the abyss   between my spirit and me are my suits
my minutes are written up raised the walls of a luciola thickness
which i admit to not knowing like the violent tissue of chromosomes
the bland abysses being embedded in my body
made of cosmogonic lava matter and nerve
of domestic convulsion
of friendly tumor in the shape of a medicinal crater
a substance made of corpuscles of daily existence
provided with the time needed for each pulsation
and each one of them is at the same time an atom
an angel a work of art a human being
a god of thick solar mane
i am aware of this equilibrium daily
of a bow dangerously drawn
to which i am sentenced by an idea on the verge of being shot

CON MALOS MODALES

WITH BAD MANNERS

con malos modales   soy tu apariencia interna y externa
tu verdadero ser tu virus tu extrema unción
el caníbal en que me convierto
sin esperar mucho tiempo en los parques lustrosos
me envilezco sin ninguna razón
me envilezco por nada me envilezco más pronto que el odio
que actúa bajo el efecto del ácido corrosivo
hago de tu traje mi mejor máscara
te muestro una rosa dentro de un volcán
bebo para ejercitar mi tino en la escama de la boa
en fin encuentro que me tardo que he perdido mis días
que no hay diferencia entre la potencia y el deseo entre el deseo
y el acto entre el acto y el crimen
huyo de mis antepasados los encuentro en todas partes
en los volúmenes de historia en mis camisas en el barniz de la mesa
y en la mesa misma en los paréntesis de lóbulos abiertos
en las carnicerías en los perros de presa en los ramos de flores
en la página 4

with bad manners   i am your internal and external appearance
your true being your virus your extreme unction
the cannibal i become
not a long wait in shiny parks
i debase myself for no reason
i debase myself for nothing i debase myself faster than hate
which acts under the effects of corrosive acid
i make your suit my best mask
i show you a rose inside a volcano
i drink to practice my aim at the boa scales
in sum i find i am running late i have lost my days
there isn't a difference between potency and desire between desire
and act between act and crime
i flee my ancestors i find them everywhere
in the history volumes in my shirts in the table varnish
and on the table itself in the open lobe parentheses
in butcher shops in dogs of prey in bunches of flowers
on page 4

cuarzo   mis salidas humillantes a una edad difícil de soportar
arrastrando mi infancia con sigilo de liebre asustada por el fondo
de una habitación alumbrada con tus ojos de viscosa luciérnaga
mis retornos a una edad menos salvaje como celebrando una victoria
al fondo de mi sangre y la estrella de los muertos que alumbraba
la batida contra el caimán y los caballos descuartizados
cuyo lomo hedía como la muerte de un cetáceo
mis razones de hombre libre en la proa una hora antes de amanecer
y los gavilanes cuyos ojos salados arrancábamos para diversión
en las embarcaciones que efectuaban sobre su espinazo de ballena
la lectura del mar
los vidrios removiendo alguna extraña confesión
esos restos de licor agrio entre los pólipos
y el miedo que gibaba la nuca del celador y los puñales
que resplandecían en las fiestas de lámparas arborescentes los arcos
de bambúes tendidos para el recibimiento el temor a los fantasmas
de viejas goletas hundidas en brindis
de estrellas de mar

quartz   my humiliating exits at an age difficult to bear
dragging my childhood with the slyness of a frightened hare through the
    back
of a room lit by your viscous firefly eyes
my returns at a less savage age like celebrating a victory
in the depths of my blood and the star of the dead illuminating
the battue against the caiman and carved-up horses
whose backs stunk like a cetacean death
my free man reasons at the bow an hour before dawn
and the sparrowhawks whose salty eyes we pulled out for fun
in the vessels that carried out the sea reading
over their whale spines
glass stirring up some strange confession
those remains of bitter alcohol among the polyps
and the fear curved the guard's nape and the daggers
shone in the festivals of arborescent lights the bamboo
arches laid out for the reception the fear of the phantoms
of old drowned schooners in toasts
to starfish

el magma debe retornar   el mundo como una habitación
demasiado sola desde donde admiro los volcanes
el receso justo de sus lavas sobre un balneario lujoso
he vendido mi ángel
lo he matado con torpe espada sin lavar
me ha cegado lo invisible
soporto en silencio mi trabajo de investigador solamente
preocupado por la carne que marcha solo por un desierto
me doy cuenta de un retorno que no es sino
un descenso de navajas sobre mi cráneo
de naipe suspendido sobre el ojo de un culpable

the magma must return   the world like a room
too alone where i admire the volcanoes
the exact recess of their lavas on a luxury spa
i have sold my angel
i have killed it with a clumsy knife unwashed
what is invisible has blinded me
in silence i bear my research only
concerned with the flesh that goes alone through a desert
i become aware of a return that is nothing more than
a descent of jackknives along my cranium
a playing card hovering above the eye of a guilty one

en memoria del ángel   nada tengo que ver con lo que he sido
ni con lo que ahora mismo soy existo simplemente
mejor dicho se me da permiso para existir se me cambia de sitio
se me asigna otro cuerpo a menudo familiar pero sin embargo
demasiado estrecho para mi espíritu
se me asesina
"sé lo que tú quieras pero al menos elige" me dicen
mejor dicho me gritan al oído manteniendo mi garganta
tensa bajo la punta del cuchillo

me confío a la fórmula del cieno de las grandes avenidas
al alcohol de las madréporas

si tan sólo se me deja abrir la boca para gritar
si tan sólo se me deja huir para encontrar el abismo
que se abre ahí delante como otra boca
lo terrible emana siempre de un golpe de azar
pero los acontecimientos esperan se amontonan
se precipitan en cascada queriendo todos suceder a la vez
tocan a mi puerta penetran en mi cuerpo
se instalan en mi piel como una sustancia renovada
y a la vez muerta que mi ser acepta sin vacilar
su sentido proviene del golpe de agua que arrastra al pez
aún estoy allí
no hago nada

mis pasos tienen seguramente un origen
no obstante no sabrían adónde ir
yo mismo no lo sé me confío demasiado he cometido
un error de cálculo
en efecto el retorno debía hacerlo a toda carrera
si he llegado ahora es solamente para volver a empezar
una vez que tomaba impulso era como el pájaro que regresa
muerto por exceso de confianza en el vuelo
es desconsolador

in memory of the angel   i have nothing to do with what i have been
or with what i am right now i simply exist
or rather i have been given permission to exist I am moved around
given another body often familiar but still
too narrow for my spirit
i am killed
"be what you want but at least choose" they tell me
or rather they scream it in my ear keeping my throat
tense at knifepoint

i entrust to myself the mud formula of the great avenues
the alcohol of the madrepores

if they'd only let me open my mouth to scream
if they'd only let me flee to find the abyss
opening up ahead like another mouth
what is terrible always arises from a stroke of luck
but the occurrences await amass
rush in cascades all wanting to happen at the same time
they knock on my door penetrate my body
install in my skin like a substance at once renovated
and dead that my being accepts unwavering
their sense comes from the rush of water that sweeps the fish along
i am still there
i do nothing

my steps surely have an origin
but they wouldn't know where to go
i don't even know i am reckless i have made
a miscalculation
sure enough the return should have happened at full speed
if i am here now it's only to go back to the start
once i had the impetus it was like a bird returning
dead by excess trust in flight
it is distressing

debajo de cada nuevo intento no hay más que un mar furioso
que vuelve a la calma en cuanto yo desaparezco

me adiestro en cada uno de mis defectos perfeccionándolos
en toda su extensión afilándolos hasta que adquieren
ese brillo repulsivo de mis dientes que se disponen a saltar
En ese instante la duda nace en mí ¿soy la presa o el verdugo?
debería escoger ahora mismo
mas definitivamente no puedo elegir
es imposible me digo
                    y salto

beneath each new attempt there's nothing but a furious sea
turning calm as soon as i disappear

i train myself in each of my flaws perfect them
to their full extent sharpen them until they acquire
the repulsive glow of my teeth which are inclined to attack
at that moment doubt is born in me am i the prey or the executioner?
i ought to choose right now
but actually i can't
it's impossible i tell myself
and jump

los horizontes son nuestros brazos   en el dominio de las perspectivas los horizontes son nuestros brazos apenas hay algo que hacer no podrías imaginarte en otro sitio sin que no te invada una especie de vértigo fatal las distancias son demasiado largas para la esperanza los cambios se suceden hacia abajo así la verdadera causa del sueño no está en ti sino en los gusanos ellos piensan por ti vigilan mientras tú duermes duermes los lugares existen por fuerza de las costumbres sólo podrías hallarlos en los mapas y ni siquiera en los mapas en cuanto das un paso convencido de poder alcanzarlos ruedas abatido hacia el abismo de nada me sirven mis brazos mis piernas mis largos dedos provistos de aspas parecidas a navajas ante mis propios ojos me pierdo de vista a mí mismo no me conozco estoy abolido un muñón miserable ha tomado mi sitio

the horizons are our arms   within the dominion of perspectives the horizons are our arms there's almost nothing you can do you can't picture yourself anywhere else without a fatal vertigo taking you over the distances are too far for hope the changes happen downward so the real cause of dream isn't in you it's in the worms they think for you watch over you while you sleep sleep places exist out of habit you can only find them on maps and not even on maps right as you take a step convinced you can reach them you roll down into the abyss my arms are useless my legs my long fingers equipped with razor-like blades are useless i lose sight of myself before my very own eyes i don't recognize me i am wrecked a wretched stump has taken my place

EL INVISIBLE SALE DE CASA

THE INVISIBLE MAN LEAVES
THE HOUSE

una vez que se toma el sombrero la despedida es cosa inevitable
            entonces el invisible sale de casa ¿volverá?
las palabras se juegan la vida se cruzan acertijos como cartas
que otra vez son espadas y así termina el último acto
pistola en mano pero no antes de que los invitados lleguen
trayendo flores con esos ademanes discretos que preceden
a la noche de boda y aun con la gota de vino que salpica
en sus ojos frescos y aun el mismo féretro que muy pronto
se ha cansado de esperar que ya a nadie sorprende
pues necesita más espacio para respirar más hormigas
                                        que obliguen su paso
y los amigos deben volver han vuelto ya están en casa
sentados con el cuello de la camisa más brillante que mortaja
o caminando de puntillas para no hacerse notar
andando de esa manera distinguida que no oculta el brillo
de los zapatos detrás de la mesa de comer
mas alguien debe hacer el resto cuando el pesado traje
se queda sin cuerpo colgando como res muerta en los ganchos
recoger los vasos rotos poner la cabeza en grandes negocios
hacer las cuentas llenar nuevamente las tazas de café
que propagan un amable ruido de platos por toda la casa
dar las buenas noches como a nuevo inquilino sin olvidar
esa flor en el ojal que de pronto asusta más que el muerto
despacio despacio puesto que la tierra necesita de alimento
y suponemos que todo lo que hagas con ese cuerpo
demasiado recto lo harán a su vez con el tuyo para conformidad
otra vez ese cuerpo enganchado en la noche
que no sabría leer su suerte en la hoja que come un bachaco
eso mismo que te preocupa mientras ladeas tu cabeza
y echas más azúcar en el café arrojando con tu pala tanta tierra
tanta tierra fría sobre el montón que sobresale alegremente
como si se acabara de sembrar el arbolito
y después te callas te dan por muerto
y después te tienes que sentar guardando un silencio conveniente
que da náuseas y apagan las luces y no te mueves y sientes
bajo tus párpados crecer los pelos del muerto cavando en tu frente

once a hat's been picked up a goodbye is inevitable
        so the invisible man leaves the house will he be back?
words risk their lives crossing riddles like cards
which are once again swords and this is how the final act ends
pistol in hand but not before the guests arrive
bringing flowers with those discrete signs that foretell
the wedding night and even with the wine drop splatter
in their fresh eyes and even the very coffin quite soon
tired of waiting which no longer surprises anyone
since it needs more space to breathe more ants
                                        to force the way
and friends ought to come back they are back they are home now
sitting there with their shirt collars brighter than a shroud
or tiptoeing around to not be heard
walking in that distinguished way that doesn't hide the shine
of their shoes behind the dining table
but someone ought to do the rest when the heavy suit
is left bodyless hanging like a dead cow from a hook
pick up the broken glasses put their head in big business
crunch the numbers refill the coffee cups
that echo a pleasant sound of plates throughout the house
say goodnight like to a new tenant not forgetting
a flower in the buttonhole that is suddenly scarier than the dead man
slowly slowly since the earth needs nourishment
and we assume that all you do to this too straight
body they'll do it in turn to yours for conformity
once more this body hooked on the night
wouldn't know how to read its luck in the leaf eaten by a bachaco ant
this is exactly what's worrying you while you tilt your head back
and put more sugar in your coffee shoveling so much dirt
so much cold dirt onto the pile that happily swells
as if the tiny tree had just been planted
and then you shut up they've given you up for dead
and then you have to sit down keeping a convenient sick-to-the-stomach
silence and they turn off the lights and you stay still and under your eyelids
you feel the dead man's hairs growing they dig into your forehead

como un agua lustral y después estamos sobre la alfombra
en esa postura intransigente que molesta como cuerda
demasiado ceñida a una garganta
si regresas al otro día mucho tiempo se habrá ido
en la amapola muerta las sillas colocadas reflexivamente
ante la mesa donde se jugaba anoche una partida
tu retrato que se pudre sin que se altere el rostro
teje la araña lo que desteje el reloj mucho tiempo violento
marcado por el vuelo de la mariposa negra en el cuarto
mucho tiempo que no se sabe si ha pasado realmente
por tu rostro o por el lomo del caballo que otro amo
con su ojo engorda al día siguiente
un día desfigurado por la lluvia en que las hormigas

                                         cargan la hoja de plátano

like holy water and then we're on the rug
in that uncompromising position which is annoying like a rope
too tight at the throat
if you come back the next day a lot of time will have gone
into the lifeless poppy the chairs reflexively placed
at a table where a round was played last night
your portrait rotting your face unaltered
the spider spins what the clock unspins so much violent time
marked by the flight of the black butterfly in the room
so much time that may or may not have actually passed
by your face or the horse's back fattened by
another owner's eye the next day
a day mutilated by the rain when ants
                              carry the banana leaf

DESCENDIENTE DE AHAB

DESCENDENT OF AHAB

para un público enfermo
  ávido de ver la sangre corriendo en lugar del agua
llegado el caso sé hacer la victima
      y canto en mi agonía entre dos fuegos
vuelve vuelve oía a mi madre
      su voz me despertaba
otras veces escuchaba los aullidos de los perros
(mi público está formado exclusivamente de fieras)
escuchaba sus burlas horribles cuando aún
      mi sangre destilaba bajo el entarimado
vuelve vuelve
oía la voz cada vez más apagada
pero la palabra moría antes de haber nacido en un lugar lejano
vuelve vuelve
soy un desierto

for a sick public
    eager to see blood run instead of water
when it comes down to it i know how to play the victim
        and i sing in my agony between two fires
come back come back i'd hear my mother
      her voice would wake me up
other times listening to the dog howls
(my audience is made up exclusively of beasts)
i'd listen to her horrible teasing as
       my blood trickled down beneath the floorboards
come back come back
i'd hear the voice more and more muffled
but the word would die before being born in a distant place
come back come back
i am a desert

fin del acto   la audiencia donde al fin vas a someterte
        a una operación urgente
a una suerte de amputación de tu lado enfermo
en esa sala demasiado alta donde
            al ser cambiada de sitio
la viga cae justamente sobre tu ojo abierto
una partida de dados comienza a jugarse sigue
a las palabras de la sentencia
mas las pruebas existen
siempre han existido   están a la vista
no necesitan ser presentadas para que se te condene
inmediatamente
puesto que las descubres por todas partes
        asidas como pulpos a tu mesa
transformadas de repente en las flores
            que han enviado para el fin del acto
el péndulo interviene en la ejecución de la sentencia
señala las pautas trenza el tiempo

end of the act   the hearing where you will at last subject yourself
      to an urgent operation
to a sort of amputation of your sick side
in this abnormally tall room where
        when moved into place
the beam lands right on your open eye
a game of dice starts to play out follows
the words of the sentence
but the proof exists
it has always existed   it is in view
it doesn't need to be exhibited for you to be condemned
right away
since you find it all over the place
      attached like octopus to your table
suddenly changed to flowers
        sent for the end of the act
the pendulum takes part in carrying out the sentence
points out the guidelines braids time

el doble hace su entrada   pierdo mi tiempo dibujando monstruos
en las paredes
        de una habitación desierta
espectros que sin atreverse a entrar se asoman por la ventana
yo les hago señas los invito a que pasen
todo en vano siempre terminan escapándose
¡saludo sus sábanas de ángeles
            sus apariencias extravagantes!
es ese picotear insolente de los gavilanes
sobre las páginas de mis cuadernos al que atribuyo
el desorden que reina en mi cuarto
debo echarlos ahora mismo
después de todo mi oficio consiste en eso
monto en cólera
al cabo soporto en silencio que no se vayan jamás
siempre encuentran un sitio mejor para instalarse
mas mi cólera aumenta trepa por las paredes del cuarto
al volver descubro allí mismo a un enorme perro
seguramente hace guardia
ahora bien yo intento ganar su confianza
arrojándole las partes de mi cuerpo que aún
            no ha terminado de comerse
que aún no ha terminado de comerse

the double enters the scene   i waste my time drawing monsters
on the walls
        of a deserted room
ghosts don't risk going in but they peak through the window
i wave them over invite them to come in
all for nothing they always end up bailing
i greet their angel sheets
            their extravagant appearances!
the insolent pecking of sparrowhawks
on the pages in my notebooks is my explanation for
the disorder that reigns over my room
i should kick them out right now
after all it's my job
i fly off the handle
later i silently put up with them never leaving
they always find a better place to settle down
but my rage grows climbs the walls
i'm back and i find a giant dog right there
surely a guard dog
so i try to win him over
throwing him the parts of my body he's
            still eating
the parts he's still eating

mi vocación de actor   mi vocación de actor que toma
demasiado en serio
la representación de un crimen había sido decretada
        recuerdo muy bien la lluvia
sobre el muérdago que estrujaba en mi mano para hacer
más familiar el contacto del cuchillo
había olvidado mi nombre
me aproximaba a la casa de mis padres
            azuzado por una vocación terrible
debo ejecutar a diario números de magia
cuenta uno a uno los segundos de esos diez años
que permaneces sentado p e n o s a m e n t e
        allí ante el juez

my vocation as an actor   my vocation as an actor who takes
the performance of a crime
too seriously had been decreed
      i remember it perfectly the rain
on the mistletoe i crushed it in my hand to prepare it
for contact with the knife
i had forgotten my name
i got closer to my parents' house
            fueled by a terrible vocation
i must execute magic numbers daily
count them one by one the seconds of those ten years
when you p a i n f u l l y stay seated
            there before the judge

la venganza   todas las eventualidades que contribuyen
a la desdicha de orestes combinan su regreso
prácticamente no ha debido moverse ha estado siempre
en el palacio como príncipe o como actor el caso es
el mismo porque lo atan a las columnas
los cabos de sus nuevas víctimas
nada más que el cinabrio junto a la fosa corriente
los relevos de guardia que suceden a una hora incierta
precisamente en el momento en que ejecuta su venganza

revenge   all eventualities that contribute
to the misfortune of orestes go with his return
he practically couldn't move he's always been
in the palace like a prince or an actor it's always
the same because he's tied to the columns
by the ropes of his new victims
nothing more than cinnabar by the common grave
the changings of the guard that happen at irregular times
exactly at the moment when he executes his revenge

poste   mas cuando avanzas sientes que la cadena se ha enroscado
en tu cuello ¿qué habrá pasado? es ese instante
en el cual comprendes que no estás libre sino que por el contrario
la cadena te acerca más y más al poste
fundo tu alegría en una marcha inversa pues las cosas opinan de otro modo
suprimen tus gestos hasta ese límite intolerable en que pruebas sostenerte
con pie firme sobre un agua profunda que te envuelve

pole   but as you move forward you feel the chain becoming twisted
around your neck what could've happened? right at that instant
you grasp that you are not free but quite the opposite
the chain inches you closer and closer to the pole
i establish your happiness in reverse because things think differently they
suppress your movement up to that intolerable limit where you try to stand
firm upon the deep water that has you surrounded

escalón   estoy en el peldaño más bajo de una escalera que me conduce a donde están los otros admito que debería comenzar a subir en el acto pues no me es dado seguir aquí vacilo hasta puedo pensar la cosa es más terrible sin embargo sucede que no puedo moverme y no porque esté impedido físicamente sino porque ignoro la existencia de los peldaños intermedios si bien por otra parte distingo claramente a donde llevan

step   i'm on the lowest tread of a stairway it leads me to where the others are i admit that i ought to start climbing right away since it is not a given i'll stay here i hesitate i even think it over but it's actually worse it so happens that i can't move and not because i'm physically impaired it's because i am unaware of the existence of the middle treads although on the other hand i can clearly tell where they're going

cadena sola   y más allá al término de una vida triste el prisionero mudo ante las reglas del juego su mirada cubre la escena como una bestia que se dispone a morir quiere saber lo que hay detrás del muro y la reja mas en cualquier dirección que mire descubrirá sólo su propio rostro en los ojos del carcelero ciertamente su mundo no es pequeño ha matado sus raíces se extienden por encima de los muros crecen puede incluso moverse caminar ir hacia sí mismo por sobre la cadena

single chain   and beyond all that at the end of a sad life the prisoner silent before the rules of the game his gaze ascends the scene like a beast about to die he wants to know what's behind the wall and the bars but if he looks in any direction he'll only find his own face in the jailer's eyes of course his world is not small he has killed his roots spread over the walls they grow he can even move walk go toward himself over the chain

cuento   el sol me despertaba como a pájaro
veía los mapas en las paredes la luz que atravesaba países
nunca imaginados indicando desde la ventana los sitios
por donde empezaron a rodar mares incalculables
yo miraba a todos lados señor eran sólo sábanas
mas el diluvio oprimía mis sienes como si mil gallos
se inclinaran para narrarme al oído el fin del mundo
entonces despertaba
y qué impuro el día opuesto al sueño sobre la niebla
donde un momento antes desaparecieron los ángeles
cada cosa alumbraba como un ojo
llameaban los cuadernos los trajes los juegos
presentes de muerte que el día arrojaba a mi cara

story   the sun would wake me like a bird
i saw the maps on the walls the light moving through countries
never imagined from the window revealing the places
where incalculable seas began to roll
i looked all around reader they were just sheets
but still the deluge crushed my temples as if a thousand roosters
had bent down to whisper the end of the world in my ear
then i would wake up
and how impure the day compared to the dream upon the mist
where right before the angels had disappeared
each thing lit up like an eye
the notebooks the suits the games all in flames
death presents the day had thrown in my face

un hilo sobre el abismo   la araña tiende un hilo en el abismo
y comienzas a caminar inmediatamente sobre lo que de pronto
se curva como lomo de serpiente
estar allí sobre un pantano miserable mientras tu miedo
toma cuerpo en los aullidos de la fiera
mientras ocurre ese temblor de víctima que derrumba tu casa
una suave brisa de naipes removiendo un cráneo

a thread above the abyss   the spider spins a silk thread in the abyss
and you immediately begin to walk on what suddenly
curves like the spine of a snake
to be there above a miserable swamp while your fear
takes shape in the howls of the beast
while the victim tremor causes your house to collapse
a gentle breeze of playing cards stirring a skull

sólo comer es una empresa   entraba la multitud agitando sus dientes de dos en dos se tomaba asiento no estaba el suelo tan lleno de tabaco carnívoramente se sentaban como grandes insectos otros cerraban la boca preferirían no haber nacido guardaban silencio respetuoso miraban sobre el alto estrado a los jefes se acostaban como podían sobre sus propios huesos se subían medio muertos a la mesa pero sólo comer es una empresa la carne desaparecía antes de abrir la boca no alcanzaba para todos se peleaban a la espada con los huesos no estaba el suelo tan lleno de tabaco pero al caer del techo el escarabajo se ahogó en la cerveza

only eating is an enterprise   the crowd came in shaking their teeth two by two they took a seat the floor wasn't so full of tobacco carnivorously they sat down like giant insects others closed their mouths they would prefer to not have been born they kept a respectful silence they looked over the high podium at the bosses they went to bed as best they could upon their own bones they climbed up to the table half-dead but only eating is an enterprise the meat disappeared before they opened their mouths it was not enough for all of them they fought with swords with bones the floor wasn't so full of tobacco but when the beetle fell from the roof it drowned in beer

me levanto   cuando con mi voz he traspasado la mañana herido las carnes de los que duermen anegado sus lechos con tibia sangre sin reposo cuando me levanto y cruzo la desolada tierra misteriosa soñando realizar una hazaña imposible cuando entro en erección cuando rehago tu vida y nuevamente la arrojo como cera al volcán cuando estoy por encima de todo cuando me transformo cuando río a carcajadas cuando me embriago de muerte diaria para renacer en el rebaño cuando escucho la memoria que teje un nudo en mi garganta y de miedo contando hasta tres comienzo a gritar

i get up   when wounded i have pierced the morning with my voice
the flesh of those who sleep i am restless flooded their beds with warm
blood when i get up and cross the desolate mysterious land dreaming of
accomplishing an impossible feat when i get an erection when i remake
your life and throw it like wax into the volcano one more time when i am
above everything when i shapeshift when i laugh out loud when i get drunk
on daily death to be reborn in the flock when i hear the memory weaving
a lump in my throat and out of fear counting to three i begin to scream

jonás siempre   como jonás lleno de incertidumbre
        moré en el vientre de la ciudad
esto sucedió una vez y siempre
en las cuatro estaciones de mi vida
cuando como ismael sombríamente joven y cambiante como
un desterrado la dicha fuera de mí mismo
desesperadamente yo buscaba
la dicha no encontré bajo un cielo torpe
oyendo una orden de partir esperaba en los puertos
imaginaba aventuras incomparables sin hacerme propósito
cuanto más abría los ojos el mundo me parecía más pequeño
y así viviré bajo un cielo inmóvil sin deseos
odiando la palabra el sentimiento
las cartas de retorno
el silencio de los cactos

always jonah   like jonah full of doubt
     i dwelled in the belly of the city
this happened once and for always
at the four seasons of my life
when somberly young and changing like ismael like
a banished man happiness outside of myself
i desperately searched for
happiness i did not find it beneath a clumsy sky
hearing an order to leave i waited at the ports
i imagined incomparable adventures with no reason to
the more i opened my eyes the more the world seemed smaller
and that's how i will live beneath a stagnant sky no desires
hating the word the feeling
the return letters
the cacti silence

Malos modales
Bad Manners
(1965)

Ciudadano libre a un palmo por encima de su postura común
mostrándome tal como soy en la plenitud
de mis facultades perdidas en los potes de basura
y en los letreros que se leen cómodamente desde los mingitorios
notando que no existe otra vida ni un segundo
ni un tercer acto después del primero
curvado a la mitad de mi vida en un recodo yermo
fuera del camino público y por deseo propio lanzado
al interior de mi vaso de vino no teniendo maestro
ni alumnos ni a nadie ante quien acudir para mi defensa
ni motivos especiales grandes o pequeños para cantar
para reír para hacer todas mis necesidades juntas
y demócrata en la forma en que erupto o en la forma
en que el perro aparece tirado en la vía rápida
en la forma en que rasco mis pies uno contra el otro
a semejanza de dos automóviles que copulan
encontrándose a gran velocidad en sentidos opuestos
        con olor a colmena fúnebre
a sabiendas que conviene ser siempre el mismo
y que no vinimos únicamente para vivir
y sin ningún país por el que exista momentáneamente
la obligación o el deber de morir y pensando que algo
va a suceder cuando ya nada ocurra junto al público
que me hace perder el equilibrio en el instante más decisivo
de mi número doy un paso en falso sobre la tierra accidentada
que abre su sexo no tengo ni buenos ni malos
antecedentes pido disculpas señores
el bien y el mal cohabitan en cada partícula mía
Espléndida ciudad bendice las alcantarillas
y las cicatrices de tus muertos acércame el cuchillo
soy tu reo que empuja una piedra de centella
demasiado grande hacia el borde inalcanzable de un abismo
Y espero que esta no sea mi única oportunidad
Y espero que esta no sea mi última oportunidad
y arrullado por el canto de sirenas del pentotal nocturno
habiendo perdido la perspectiva y el sentido práctico

Free citizen just an inch above the common posture
showing myself as I am at the height
of my abilities lost in garbage cans
and signs read comfortably from urinals
noting that another life or a second
or third act doesn't exist after the first
curved in the middle of my life in a barren bend
off the public road and by its very desire flung
to the inside of my wineglass not having a teacher
or students or anyone to appeal my defense to
or special reasons great or small to sing
to laugh to do all my necessities at once
and democratic in the way I belch or in the way
a dog appears thrown in the fast lane
in the way I scratch one foot against the other
similar to two cars copulating
finding themselves at great speeds in opposite directions
      with a scent of funeral hive
knowing that it's in my best interest to always be the same
and that we did not come here only to live
and without any country to exist for momentarily
the obligation or duty to die and thinking that something
is going to happen when nothing does along with the public
which makes me lose my balance at the most decisive instant
of my number I take a false step on the uneven earth
opening its sex I don't have good or bad
prior records I beg your pardon sirs
good and evil live together in each of my particles
Splendid city bless the sewers
and the scars of your dead the knife draws near
I am your prisoner I push a huge lightning
stone toward the unreachable edge of an abyss
And I hope this won't be my only chance
And I hope this won't be my last chance
and lulled to sleep by the siren cantos of nighttime Pentothal
having lost the perspective and the common sense

pródigo en hijos cuyas bocas abiertas al unísono
constituyen mi único mi verdadero firmamento
con mis principios en alto atados a los papagayos
que caerán seguramente y mis derechos conquistados
de disfrutar el tiempo perdido en el rincón oscuro
de una cárcel yo hombre libre que emplea sus mejores ratos
en trotar cabizbajo por esta ciudad a la que arrojo
mi parentesco de larva doméstica y donde saludo
y me llevo precipitadamente las manos al vientre
retrocediendo como el cangrejo para alcanzar la eternidad
en algún hueco de mi cerebro y donde roturo
con mis dedos la yerba silenciosa de los parques
hombre libre amenazado por la bala que no se tiene tiempo
de oír y cuyo origen pierde importancia ante el color
de la mesa donde reposa el cofre con cirios a ambos
lados de la frente y casi chisporroteante
        a modo de una lágrima cayendo sobre una brasa
pierdo tiempo emerjo muerdo la zona oscura de mis párpados
cordial efímero único fluctuante
mi salvación aguarda no es posible que mi reloj sea una estrella
más cerca de mi ombligo que del cerebro
mostrándome como soy en el instante y no en la palabra
en la explosión y no en la calma excluido
por la razón que da el uso de la razón
y sentado en mi gloria relativa levantando la voz
como un ciego que agita sus puños sin ser oído por nadie
en el deseo de los tiempos mejores que se esperan
y en la esperanza de lo que se pierde
Ciudadano libre en esta ciudad no humana pero tampoco divina
donde floto tan sólo por una décima de segundo y pudiendo
esperar mucho más tiempo aún debajo de la tierra
a una edad en que nada bueno promete el tiempo

prodigious in children whose mouths open in unison
comprise my one my true firmament
with my principles on high fastened to the parrots
that will surely fall and my conquered rights
to enjoy lost time in the dark corner
of a prison I am a free man using his best moments
to trot crestfallen through this city which I hurl
my domestic larvae kin to and where I greet
and hastily bring my hands to my belly
falling back like a crab to reach eternity
in some hole in my brain and where I plow
the silent grass of the parks with my fingers
free man threatened by the bullet you don't have time
to hear and whose origin loses relevance before the color
of the table where the chest with candles sits at both
sides of my forehead and almost crackling
        like a tear falling over hot coals
I waste time I emerge bite the darkzone of my eyelids
cordial ephemeral sole fluctuating
my salvation awaits it is impossible for my watch to be a star
closer to my navel than my brain
showing me how I am in the instant not in the word
in the explosion and not in the calm excluded
by the reason that the use of reason gives
and seated in my relative glory raising my voice
like a blind man shaking his fists heard by no one
in the desire for better times to come
in the hope of what is lost
Free citizen in this city neither human nor divine
where I float only for a tenth of a second and being able
to wait much more still beneath the earth
at an age in which time promises nothing good

CONTANDO HASTA CERO

COUNTING TO ZERO

Contando hasta cero

Me habitúo a esa escritura compasiva de los individuos que dan a las cosas su verdadero nombre adoptan la postura correcta y viven fuera del error condenados a una existencia apacible Es el desvanecimiento cotidiano de quien se siente halado hacia una bocacalle mientras saluda todas las mañanas con el mismo aire grave bajando el vidrio de la ventanilla para divisar mejor ¿Qué cosa? Esa perspectiva uniforme establecida a ras de la conciencia un escritorio un punto la señal un pisapapel una ascensión que termina siempre por debajo del nivel ordinario aunque algo más lejos pero siempre más rápidamente de lo que se espera nunca demasiado tarde nunca demasiado tarde Una piedra no va más lejos dando tumbos sobre la superficie de un lago ¿Me oyes? Es el día de tu partida toma todo lo indispensable . . .

Counting to Zero

I am used to the compassionate writing of individuals who give things their real name assume the correct position and live outside error condemned to a gentle existence It is the quotidian fading of someone who feels pulled toward an intersection while each morning with the same serious gaze they say hi rolling down the window to better discern What? The uniform perspective established flush with consciousness a desk a point the sign a paperweight an ascension ending always below the normal level although somewhat further away but always quicker than expected never too late never too late A stone does not travel further tumbling over the surface of a lake Do you hear me? It is the day of your departure take everything you need . . .

Mis decisiones se encuentran demasiado cerca del fuego
Más cerca de la tierra que del cielo

Imagino mis costumbres sensatas paseándose
        en un sillón de ruedas
    a lo largo de una sala de invernadero
Pregunto si ésta es la posición más ventajosa
para descubrir a mis amigos que apoyan una pistola
                en mi axila
Procuro el desvelo eterno de las bielas
La nostalgia de infinito no sirve
        sino para acercarme más y más al suelo
Formulo una disposición poco vulnerable a mantenerme
    con la cabeza hacia abajo en equilibrio reinante
        justo entre el abismo y mis manos
El látigo es al mismo tiempo la cuerda
Finjo que tomo el arma
        Es mi confianza ciega
        Es mi confianza ciega

My decisions are too close to the fire
Closer to the earth than the sky

I picture my sensible habits strolling
        through a greenhouse
    in a wheelchair
I ask if this is the best position to be in
to catch my friends putting a gun
                        to my armpit
I seek the eternal sleeplessness of the connecting rod
The nostalgia for infinity is only good
            for getting my body closer and closer to the ground
I draw up a slightly vulnerable disposition to keep
    my head down in dominating balance
            right between the abyss and my hands
The whip is also the rope
I pretend to take the gun
        It is my blind faith
        It is my blind faith

Despierto   Sigo vivo por ese solo instante
en que descubro la situación de mi enemigo
que habita conmigo el mismo cuerpo
la misma jaula
abundo en detalles olímpicos Declino
el logro de la dicha   Todas mis grandes
    empresas naufragando en un vaso de agua
Es su suerte fatal
cuando creo andar en línea recta
me veo girando alrededor de mí mismo
Acudo ante el juez   Todas las pruebas me condenan
Despierto   Huyo pero las gradas son interminables
                                        interminables

Awake   I am still alive for that one moment
when I figure out where my enemy is located
he lives with me in the same body
the same cage
I elaborate in Olympic details I pass up
the feat of happiness   All my great
    enterprises sinking in a glass of water
It is their fatal luck
when I think I'm walking in a straight line
I see myself spinning around my body
I go before the judge   All the evidence convicts me
Awake   I run away but the grandstands are endless
                                        endless

Todas mis preocupaciones son el hilo de donde cuelgo
Si subo llegado arriba
me convierto en ese abominable sujeto
que dibuja signos cabalísticos en las paredes
    de su cerebro
Llegado arriba no sé qué hacer
  Es inútil   Ni lo alto ni lo bajo existen
Lo más alto parecería lo más profundo
Requiero la confianza en un espíritu ebrio
Sigo   Doy vueltas   No puedo escapar
    el hecho de ser siempre yo mismo
Se me suprime
A pesar de que aún para eso
    sea yo quien decida
      Señores

All my worries are the thread I hang from
If I climb to the top
I turn into that vile subject
who scrawls cabalistic signs on the walls
    of his brain
At the top I don't know what to do
    It's pointless   High or low don't exist
The highest point looks like the lowest
I need to trust a drunken mind
I keep on   I spin   I cannot escape
    the fact that I am always myself
It gets struck down
Even though I am the one who
    makes that decision too
       Sirs

Las armas invisibles

Me denuncio ante los demás como un ser valiente proclamándome del modo más heroico con toda clase de instrumentos armas blancas y armas de fuego con gestos de ciudadano orgulloso vociferando aullando y en los momentos menos felices hasta ladrando La lluvia misma me sirve de látigo para mantener a raya a una ciudad alertada ante el peligro inminente Pero si tengo miedo adquiero inmediata conciencia de mi piel Basta sólo que una sombra se descuelgue por la superficie de un espejo Y ya no pienso más que en mí El pensamiento se estira hasta ese extremo peligroso después del cual sólo le faltaría reventar Mi paciencia carece de un punto neutro cubre la distancia de regreso No puedo verme en una habitación confortable entre libros de historia adorado como un dios por mi gente En tales casos mi piel se acoge indignamente a una especie de lagarto que me habita por dentro Corro Sucede que me adhiero a la rigidez de las sillas y medio muerto me trepo al borde inferior de las mesas de comer A fin de cuentas mi miedo emana sólo de mí Soy el ciudadano culpable el origen y el fin de mi asco Siento pavor y al descubrirme bajo este aspecto repelente me lanzo detrás de mí mismo perseguido por la más espeluznante de las bestias

The Invisible Arms

I denounce myself before the others as bold proclaiming myself in the most heroic way with all kinds of instruments blades and firearms with the gestures of a proud citizen shouting howling and in the unhappiest moments even barking Rain itself is a whip for me to keep a city in line before the imminent danger But if I get scared I become immediately aware of my skin A shadow descending from a mirror surface suffices And I think only of myself Thoughts stretch toward a dangerous extreme after which they only need burst My patience lacks a neutral point covers the distance of returning I cannot see myself in a comfortable room among history books adored like a god by my people In such cases my skin indignantly shelters a kind of lizard that lives inside me I run And then I cling to the stiffness of chairs and half-dead I make my way toward the lower end of dining room tables When all is said and done my fear only emanates from me I am the guilty citizen the beginning and end of my disgust I feel terror and when I discover myself beneath this repellant appearance I throw myself behind me chased by the most horrifying of beasts

Hago un alto

Hago un alto para ver cuánto he caminado Ya no ando a grandes pasos
sino que a cada instante me detengo para apreciar la distancia recorrida El
camino siempre asciende su trayectoria se vuelve penosa como la pendiente
de un volcán y para colmo cumple una vuelta en órbita al cabo de la cual
descubro que estoy donde mismo y que aún no he partido

I Take a Break

I take a break to see how far I have walked I do not take big steps anymore but every second I stop to appreciate the distance traveled The path always goes up its trajectory turns grueling like the slope of a volcano and to top it all off it completes one revolution in orbit At the end of it I realize that I am where my body is and that I haven't left yet

Subsisto

Subsisto dentro y fuera de mí mismo
　　y en los túneles de una ciudad sin memoria
Subsisto
　　　　mas me veo sin extremidades aferrado
　　a las lianas al fondo de un acuario
Subsisto tirado en la calle
Subsisto en las hileras de fetos de jardín
Subsisto en la pérdida de tiempo
Subsisto aún sin querer subsistir
　　　　esperando la orden de salvación
　　　　y la orden de disparar
y subsisto en el gesto indiscreto del que apunta
　　　　con una daga al interior de mi ojo
Subsisto en los criaderos de larvas
Subsisto en las palabras
Subsisto en la cólera

I S u b s i s t

I subsist inside and outside of my body
  and in the tunnels of a city with no memory
Subsist
    but I see myself limbless clinging
  to the vines at the bottom of a fish tank
Subsist lying on the streets
Subsist in rows of garden fetuses
Subsist in time wasted
Subsist even when I don't want to subsist
        waiting for the salvation order
        and the gunfire order
and subsist in the nosy look of someone pointing
      a dagger at the inside of my eye
Subsist in larval hatcheries
Subsist in words
I subsist in rage

Requisitoria de los trajes vacíos

Me esfuerzo en llevar los pies sobre la cabeza
Pero es inútil
Se me otorga una mirada para ojear dentro de las vitrinas
Las cajas de basura cuya circunspección
      pone en peligro el perro que lame un traje viejo
El mínimo empeño para comer lo que no existe en la mesa
Los platos que no se han puesto
      El desayuno servido en la morgue
Las sábanas de periódicos para arroparnos
              durante la tormenta
Se me otorga un portafolio de suicida
Las cajas que se han apartado con el pie
      por simple pretexto y hasta con la elegancia de un atleta
Una simple bata
La ropa alisada el ruedo hecho el doblez
        justo en la nuez de adán
Y así yo propongo una pared donde reine un silencio duro
      como una protesta pública
      como el puño que se deja caer sobre la mesa

(Nada más que un occipucio cerca de una estatua)

Interrogation of the Empty Suits

I take great pains to place my feet over my head
But it's useless
I have been granted a glance to look in display windows
The boxes of garbage whose circumspection
        puts the dog licking an old suit in danger
The minimal ambition to eat what isn't on the table
Plates that haven't been set
        Breakfast served in the morgue
Sheets of newspaper to tuck us in
                        during the storm
I have been granted a suicide briefcase
The boxes have been kicked away
        with a simple pretext and even the elegance of an athlete
A simple housecoat
Smooth clothing the hem sewn the crease
                right up against the Adam's apple
And so I propose a wall where hard silence reigns
        like a public protest
        like a fist falling on a table

(Nothing more than an occiput near a statue)

RELEVO DE GUARDIA

CHANGING OF THE GUARD

Relevo de guardia

Veo frecuentemente en las paredes de mi cuarto fantasmas que tienen mi propio largo que ríen con mi risa que parpadean con mi único ojo sano y me llaman con una voz tímida y desesperadamente mía Me hago a la idea de que no existo Tomo una resolución comparto una existencia suicida Doy unos pasos y ruedo por las escaleras Sucede que es sólo una manera de empequeñecerme hasta quedar limitado a mis propios pies Pies obligados a tamborilear sobre una superficie curva que nada saben del resto del cuerpo manos que se me han extraviado y que sin darse tregua aún me ahogan Sólo soy esa porción de mí mismo que no alcanza a existir en ninguna cosa finalmente reducida a un golpe de sábana

—Insensato me digo tú no puedes huir sin dejar un rastro de sangre en la ventana

Esa es la señal

Relaciono todas las cosas Vivo bajo permiso de muerte

Changing of the Guard

I see ghosts on the walls of my room all the time they are the same size as me they laugh like me blink with my one good eye call out to me with a voice timidly desperately mine I convince myself I do not exist I make a decision I share a suicidal existence I take a few steps and fall down the stairs Turns out it's just a way to make me smaller until I have shrunken down to just my feet Feet forced to drum on a curved surface they don't know about the rest of the body hands gone astray still drowning me relentlessly I am just the piece of myself that doesn't manage to exist in anything else finally reduced to the snap of a sheet

—Fool I tell myself you can't run away without leaving a trail of blood on the window

That is the sign

I connect everything I live under a death warrant

Paisajes subterráneos

Un espacio ante el cual lo imprevisible nace de la falta
        de confianza en el vuelo
Como quien pone sus ojos a cubierto del deshielo atroz
        debajo de un paisaje suburbano
        que el relámpago mantiene asido como si se tratara del
                mango de una espada
A manera de serpiente tal vez
            Aquello que está depositado en el camino
para que despierte la fiera cuando pasemos de largo
        suprime siempre todo exceso de coraje
Exige el grado de tensión de la cadena en el cuello
Un cubo de granito firme alrededor

Suponte que vieras en rápida sucesión
        de planos geométricos la extraordinaria fijeza
    de los fragmentos de conciencia que enceguecen
            brillan y se apagan sin dejar rastros
Al azar
Tendrías una imagen exacta en el extremo de su enfermedad

El odio que hemos engendrado al punto de que cristalice en una piedra
preciosa por la cual nos disputamos para descubrir al fin que se trata de una
granada de mano
Nuestro paisaje mutilado arena regada en unos labios mudos los brazos
dando a entender que algo ajeno al cuerpo los mueve en los matorrales entre
sexos abatidos que giran como aspas motivo de escarnio para los pájaros

Subterranean Landscapes

A space where the unforeseeable is born out of a lack
    of trust in flight
Like someone covering their eyes from the atrocious thaw
    beneath a suburban landscape
    held by lightning as if it were a
               sword handle
Like a snake maybe
        What is dumped on the road
so the wild beast awakens when we go by
    always eliminates every excess of courage
Demands a neck chain's level of tension
A firm granite cube surrounding

Suppose you saw in a rapid succession
    of geometric planes the extraordinary fixedness
  of the fragments of consciousness blinding
      glowing and extinguishing without a trace
Randomly
You would have an exact image in the far end of its sickness

The hate we have engendered to the point it crystallizes in a precious stone
that we argue over only to discover it is a hand grenade
Our mutilated landscape sand scattered to some silent lips the arms
suggesting something foreign to the body moves them in thickets among
abject sexes spinning like blades a motive for bird scorn

Bajo nuevo aviso

En un paisaje solo sin árboles ni ciudades
    si hablas te pierdes
Hay un momento en que la niebla que llevas en el ojo
    ocasiona una falsa noción de equilibrio
Entonces
    te alejas cuando en realidad tienes la impresión
    de estar más cerca del incendio del cual huyes
    con pasos seguros pero inversos a tu deseo de salvación
    Cuando en realidad deberías volver sobre tus pasos
Hay un momento en que mirarse al espejo saca de quicio
    supone hechos graves como la erosión de las montañas
Se va haciendo oscuro a mediodía
Se quiebra el cristal por su cuenta y huye la araña
Ya no se sabría lo que puede ocurrir
    Un exceso de imprevisión en los relojes
    es causa de calamidades públicas
Hay un momento demasiado vacío para la existencia de las sillas
Hay una vigilia a la que no perturba la circunstancia
    de continuar de pie junto a un cuadrado tan estrecho
    que no deja pasar nuestra mirada
El mundo adquiere allí el roce del dardo
     expuesto a la acción del fuego
El sol cabe dentro de una botella que se tira al agua
    Hay de todo La persuasión los drenajes Los juegos de azar
                     el día y la noche
Hay una tierra arrasada cuyas grietas
    imitan muy bien la presentación de la carne viva
Hay la horizontalidad que deviene la postura de confianza
Hay el ojo que muerde la zona oscura de los párpados
    en un paisaje solo sin árboles ni ciudades
Si hablas te pierdes

Under New Notice

In a lonely landscape no trees no cities
        if you speak you get lost
There is a moment when the haze you carry in your eye
        causes a false sense of balance
Then
        you move away when actually you have the impression
        of getting closer to the fire you are trying to escape
        with sure steps but also the opposite of your desire for salvation
        When actually you ought to retrace your steps
There is a moment when looking at yourself in the mirror vexes
        supposes grave acts like the erosion of mountains
It gets dark at midday
The glass breaks by itself and the spider flees
Who knows what could happen
        An excess of improvidence in the clocks
        is the reason for public calamities
There is a moment too empty for the existence of chairs
There is a vigil untroubled by the circumstance
        of continuing on foot alongside a square so narrow
        that it won't let our glances go by
There the world acquires the dart grazing
            exposed to direct fire
The sun fits in a bottle thrown to the water
        There's everything Persuasion drains Games of chance
                                    day and night
There is a land laid to waste whose fissures
        mimic perfectly the appearance of living flesh
There is the horizontal zone becoming the position of trust
There is the eye biting the darkzone of eyelids
        in a lonely landscape no trees no cities
If you speak you get lost

Ciudad sola

Al llegar el viajero busca alojarse en el más antiguo hotel sin siquiera percatarse de que la ciudad fue abandonada desde hace mucho tiempo Y es que esa impresión de ruina y soledad que descubre por todas partes resulta apenas comparable con su tristeza de visitante Observando las calles cualquiera diría que las casas continúan ocupadas las tiendas abiertas la vida a punto de comenzar después de una noche de fiesta Pero no La ciudad está deshabitada desde hace mucho tiempo

Un hongo húmedo y violáceo brota en la madera de las puertas por cuyos orificios las sabandijas se esfuerzan en penetrar a los salones principales La yerba ocupa el sitio de las camas follaje seco y tibio bajo la viga carcomida desde donde los techos descienden trazando círculos negros A ciertas horas el mar se introduce a los patios de las mansiones deposita macizos de coral y conchas de moluscos al pie de los zócalos y como respetuoso del linaje con un discreto bamboleo se retira de las habitaciones señoriales donde han ido acumulando los restos de una materia viscosa y blanda En la linde más allá de las últimas casas comienza el desierto Sopla un viento punzante sobre la plaza pública en cuyo centro casi cubierta por un montículo de arena emerge la cabeza del prócer Es desde luego una forma de morir lentamente bajo el golpe de esa brisa grave que al mismo tiempo descubre las tumbas donde descansan codo con codo los habitantes

Aquí en esta ciudad sola el viajero ha tomado la determinación de instalarse

Lonely City

When he arrives the traveler tries to stay in the oldest hotel doesn't even notice the city was abandoned long ago The impression of ruin and solitude he finds everywhere is barely comparable with his visitor sadness Watching the streets anyone would say the houses are still occupied stores open life at the point of beginning after a night of celebration But no The city has long been deserted

A humid violaceous fungus sprouts in the wooden doors The bugs strain to infiltrate main rooms through their orifices Grass takes the place of beds dry warm foliage beneath the eaten-away beam roofs descend from there tracing black circles At certain times the sea slips into the mansion gardens leaving behind masses of coral and mollusk shells at the foot of socles and as if respectful of lineage with a discreet swaying retreats from lordly rooms where the remains of a viscous smooth matter has built up At the edge beyond the last houses begins the desert A stabbing wind blows over the public plaza In the middle almost covered by a knoll of sand emerges the great leader's head Naturally it is a way to die slowly beneath the gust of a grave breeze which also reveals the tombs where elbow to elbow rest the inhabitants

Here in this lonely city the traveler is determined to stay

Una coincidencia

Suponte que vieras una botella en medio del mar demasiado lejos para pensar en buscarla Suponte que el hecho no tuviese importancia y sin embargo te arrojas sin pensarlo dos veces al mar ¿Con qué objeto? Pues viéndolo bien no se trata de un suceso real sino de un sueño uno de estos sueños a menudo hostiles y por otra parte tan verdaderos que frecuentemente te hacen pensar que sólo tu existencia es realmente un sueño Suponte que fueras tú mismo eso que flota deriva y ondula sin destino fijo como un barco de papel en medio de un torrente Suponte que te faltara valor para despertar para hacer algo por ti mismo para inclinarte a recoger esos restos exangües de tu cuerpo en el mar . . .

A Coincidence

Suppose you saw a bottle out at sea too far away to even think of going after it Suppose this fact didn't matter and just the same without a second thought you dove into the sea Why? Well on second thought this didn't really happen it was a dream one of those often hostile dreams that in fact are so real they make you think all the time that your own existence is actually a dream Suppose you were that thing floating drifting and undulating aimlessly like a paper boat in the middle of a torrent Suppose you didn't have the courage to wake up to do something for yourself to bend down to pick up those bloodless remains of your body in the sea . . .

Los espectáculos banales
dan a la multitud bien vestida
        un aire demasiado lóbrego
                        monótono
Un furioso tiempo con rugido de león
y mirada de doncella muda
                        señala el camino
indica el sitio donde no habrá nada
Un tiempo apropiado para oír
el canto de la lluvia
en medio de una catástrofe pública
En una ciudad de espaldas al cielo
puesta contra la pared
llevada a la sala de tortura
sometida a la prueba de la parafina
confiada a los perros
        y por cuya avenida mayor
camina el ciego a mediodía

Banal spectacles
give the well-dressed crowd
    an air excessively somber
                monotonous
A furious time with a lion's roar
and the glance of a voiceless damsel
              points the way
shows the spot where there will be nothing
An appropriate time to hear
the rain song
in the middle of a public catastrophe
In a city with its back to the sky
up against the wall
taken to the torture room
submitted to the paraffin test
entrusted to the dogs
    and on whose major avenue
walks the blind man at midday

CACERÍA

HUNT

Me llevan como a una bestia doméstica a un sitio de reclusión a uno de estos dispensarios nocturnos de los cuales ha desaparecido toda actitud para el amor Se me conduce al patio interno a través de un sistema de gradas relucientes movidas desde arriba por grandes poleas que imitan con sus ruidos la caída de una enorme cascada A medida que descendemos observo un recinto circular (extraordinariamente habitado) que rodean altas paredes y en cuyo centro hay una fuente El agua surge allí con ese sonido característico de los que piden auxilio debajo del océano En estas circunstancias no puedo aproximarme a la fuente ¡tal es la multitud que se amontona y riñe por alcanzarla! No debe inquietarme puesto que por todos los indicios lejos de aplacar la sed esta agua la renueva seca los labios quema las entrañas Y es que ella parece brotar no de la tierra sino de la garganta de las víctimas cuyo olor a sangre asciende desde el otro patio ¿De cuál patio? Estoy demasiado cerca para comprenderlo Me dispongo a beberla Su color es rojo Su color es rojo

Like a tamed beast they take me to a place of seclusion to one of those nocturnal dispensaries where all the love attitude has disappeared I am led to the inside courtyard through a system of shiny steps moved from above by giant pulleys that sound like an enormous waterfall As we go down I take note of a circular enclosure (amazingly inhabited) surrounded by high walls with a fountain in the middle The water bubbles up there with a sound characteristic of those begging for help beneath the ocean Under these circumstances I cannot get closer to the fountain such is the crowd that gathers and fights to reach it! It shouldn't worry me since by all indications far from quenching thirst this water restores it dries the lips burns the insides And it seems to not spring from the ground but from the throats of victims the smell of their blood rises from the other courtyard Which courtyard? I am too close to grasp it I am about to drink It is red It is red in color

El prisionero de su conciencia

Un hombre a quien hemos condenado a muerte manteniéndolo en una situación de aislamiento tal que le resulta imposible conocer las circunstancias extrañas que motivaron su condena

Un muro muy alto lo sustrae por completo de esa ciudad en la que ha vivido y por la cual tan sólo experimenta ahora una gran repugnancia La ocupación principal que hemos dado al prisionero consiste en obligarlo a pasearse sin descanso a través de lo que visto de más cerca resulta ser un laberinto cuyo espacio interno imita exactamente las circunvoluciones de su cerebro

Un condenado a quien hemos dado muerte . . .

The Prisoner of His Conscience

A man we have sentenced to death is held in isolation so that it's impossible for him to know about the strange circumstances behind his conviction
A very high wall cuts him off completely from the city where he lived and now only repulses him The main occupation we have given this prisoner is to force him to restlessly pace around what on closer inspection turns out to be a labyrinth whose inside space exactly matches the convulsions of his brain
A convicted man we have put to death . . .

Órbitas separadas

Lo que arrastra a los cuerpos hacia abajo no es tanto el peso de la piedra
como el desmedido amor que los seres sienten por la tierra
Por otra parte la fuerza que podría reunir a dos cuerpos diferentes es la
misma que los retiene para que no se unan jamás En esto radica el principio
de contradicción
Pues ellos van a su encuentro utilizando órbitas separadas
Pruebo hablar de un punto de unión demasiado análogo

Separate Orbits

What drags the bodies down isn't so much the weight of the stone as the excessive love that beings feel for the earth
On the other hand the force that could bring two different bodies together is the same one that holds them back so that they can never join Herein lies the principle of contradiction
So they go to their encounter using separate orbits
I try to speak of a joining point that is too analogous

Si he avanzado hacia adelante ha sido sólo en virtud de la idea del deslizamiento progresivo de mi cuerpo mecido al borde de un abismo Cambio de posición con la luz siguiendo el movimiento retráctil de mis tentáculos Extraño medio de locomoción después de todo avanzo inmóvil de modo larvario sin despegar las patas ni un milímetro del suelo—igual que la babosa Y no se piense en un suelo habitual firme como los empedrados Por el contrario se trata de un terreno poroso soñoliento y blando como la sustancia que cabe dentro de un cráneo expuesto a la furia de los vendavales Yo permanecía aferrado a las antenas de mis deseos Reptaba deslizándome a lo largo de la imagen fosforescente de todos mis actos frustrados Mis decisiones eran tomadas en un lugar ajeno a mí mismo para brindarme un punto de apoyo que no fuera inmediatamente absorbido por el barro Al fin y al cabo lo que llamé mi meta era el sitio desde donde nunca partía

If I have made any progress it has only been by virtue of the idea of the gradual gliding of my body swayed on the edge of an abyss I switch positions with the light following the retractable movement of my tentacles Strange means of locomotion after all I move motionlessly larvally without lifting my feet a single millimeter from the ground—just like a slug And reader don't imagine the usual ground hard like cobblestones Quite the opposite it's a porous terrain sleepy and soft like the substance that fits inside a skull open to the fury of windstorms I clung to the antennae of my desires I slid along the phosphorescent image of all my frustrated acts My decisions were made in a place foreign to me so I had a point of support that wouldn't get instantly absorbed by the mud At the end of it all what I called my objective was the place I never left

Debo decir

A qué velocidad desconfío de la fiera dejada libre en un parque de la ciudad mientras huyo sin poder avanzar un solo paso como si cada lóbulo siguiera fijo en un poste de hacer blanco Intento abrir los corazones son puertas cerradas Viéndolo bien nunca han existido Mi grito solo me denuncia a mí mismo Descubre un hueco donde nadie responde Para qué me van a oír Si yo había salido por un instante de esa habitación estrecha a manera de caja toráxica que en resumidas cuentas era mi propia vida Debo decir Comenzar mi vida donde ha terminado En alguna parte de mi cuerpo yo asistía a una extraña fiesta Horadaba mis párpados buscando una salida pero noté que mis ojos continuaban cerrados Es inútil en verdad ellos no siguen ahí No me pertenecen Ya vuelvo dije (asustado como el que se aleja del lugar donde se ha cometido un crimen) Pero huía sin poder avanzar un solo paso como quien desconfía de la fiera dejada libre en un parque Horrorizado al descubrirme a mí mismo bajo un cuerpo repelente Delante de mí había un muro y detrás una reja y más allá una reja y después un muro Al despertar me sentía arrastrado por el vértigo de una ángel que se apodera de una espada No importa Tómala es tu arma preferida

I Should Say

How quickly I grow weary of the beast set free in a city park while I escape unable to take a single step forward as if each earlobe was still stuck to a pole for target practice I try to pry open the hearts they are closed doors Then again they've never been real My scream only reveals me Finds a hole where nobody responds Why should they listen to me If for a second I'd left that room narrow like a ribcage it was in a nutshell my own life I should say To begin my life where it ended I attended a strange party in some part of my body I pierced my eyelids looking for a way out but I realized my eyes stayed shut It's useless actually they aren't there anymore They don't belong to me I'll be right back I said (scared like someone walking away from a crime scene) But I fled unable to take a single step forward like someone who's weary of the beast set free in a park Horrified to find myself under a repulsive body There was a wall in front of me and behind it a fence and beyond that a fence and then a wall When I woke up I felt dragged by the vertigo of an angel seizing a sword It doesn't matter Take it it is your weapon of choice

De transformaciones

Es triste continuar despedazado sin poder ser otra cosa que un jirón de materia atraída hacia abajo recuperada siempre por una fuerza extraña a ella Me diluyo en gestos cuya mansedumbre oculta la realidad ominosa de los modales No puedo negar que ya no soy un héroe ni negarme a las voces oscuras que pronuncian mi nombre tras una puerta que al abrirla da de repente al abismo Ella provee una verdad ciega una suerte de equilibrio sin punto de llegada habita una corteza enferma bajo la cual comienzo a vivir una muerte particularmente diaria Y sin embargo yo era el afortunado Tenía prisa por llegar siendo el primero Me celebraban ceñían mi garganta con mapas de los países que debían salir de inmediato a conquistar Me he transformado Soy otro Y si mi cuerpo carece de superficie no es a causa de que el espíritu se encuentre mejor flotando al aire libre sino porque yo mismo estoy vacío y vacía cada palabra vacíos los nombres y vacías las miradas de las estatuas donde una vez soñé hallarme

On Transformations

It's sad to keep on torn to pieces unable to be anything other than a shred of matter pulled downward always picked up by a force foreign to it I dissolve into gestures whose gentleness hides the ominous reality of manners I cannot deny that I am no longer a hero or deprive myself of the dark voices that say my name behind a door When opened it suddenly leads to the abyss It provides a blind truth a kind of balance with no point of arrival inhabits a sick crust I start to live an especially daily death under it And yet I was the lucky one I was in a hurry to get there to be the first They celebrated me covered my throat with maps of the countries they were to set out to conquer immediately I am transformed I am another And if my body lacks a surface it is not because my spirit is better floating in the open air but because I myself am empty and empty is every word empty the names and empty the looks from the statues where I once dreamt of finding myself

Demandas clemencia sabiendo que es inútil Supones que todo está en su sitio Después comprendes que lo que llamas "justo sitio" es sólo la forma cómo las cosas se conjuran para precipitarte para aplastarte Pides un espacio particular y obtienes el caos más informe que sin dilación reconoces como tu único espacio como tu única morada Te educas Te dispones a ser bueno Reduces tu existencia a algo menos que un enigma descifrado sobre el muro interior de un edificio desierto Divides tu cuerpo en dos partes igual es que se cierran sobre la médula como los dos cuerpos de un baúl de feria Ordenas el desalojo de tus órganos de tu cráneo vaciado como un ojo sobre una roca

eres el primero que interviene para causarte una muerte rápida Ordenas de mayor a menor las arrugas en que te ahogas cuando se derrama el vaso Ordenas la impostura Los días de excursión Las páginas en blanco Las decisiones finales que impiden tu decisión última

You demand clemency knowing it's useless You suppose that everything is in its place Afterward you understand that what you call "right place" is just the way things conspire to hurl you to crush you You ask for a particular space and get the most shapeless chaos that you unhesitatingly recognize as your only home You teach yourself You are willing to be good You reduce your existence to something less than an enigma deciphered on the inside wall of a deserted building You divide your body in two equal parts that close over the marrow like the two bodies in a fair coffer You order the ousting of your organs of your brain emptied like an eye over a rock

you are the first to intervene to cause yourself a quick death You order from greatest to smallest the wrinkles you drown in when the glass overflows You order the imposture Travel days Blank pages Final decisions impeding your last decision

Las contradicciones sobrenaturales

The Supernatural Contradictions

(1967)

RELEVO DE GUARDIA

CHANGING OF THE GUARD

Decisiones

Entre su vida y sus actos no hay más
    que el paso que nunca ha dado

Su avance es lento como conviene
    a la pérdida del equilibrio

Hace un alto cuando debería haber llegado

Toma los atajos miserables jamás la vía pública

Sus fracasos se resienten de una penosa verticalidad

Aparta los hechos con los pies

Ama tan sólo lo que el azar y la lógica
    se niegan a retribuirle

Se disuelve en disyuntivas del tamaño
    de una bola de fuego

Su espíritu no ha llevado alas ni siquiera en el sueño

Su pan no tiene remedio
    Es de consumo público

Su habla es el silencio de los perros

Se aleja del abismo en dirección al peligro

Se aleja del peligro en dirección al abismo

Su desesperación es visible a vuelo de pájaro

Posee lo que le arrebatan para arrojarlo a las fieras

Debe recomenzar a diario su existencia
    obligado a compartirla consigo mismo

Su continuo bajar la guardia

El esplendor de la tormenta es su estado de éxtasis

Su verdad rota como caña
    o más bien como pozo de agua oscura

Tiene la grandeza de lo que anda a rastras por el suelo

Decisions

Between his life and his acts there is nothing more
    than the step he's never taken

His progress is slow as is appropriate
    for the loss of balance

Takes a break when he should have arrived

Takes miserable shortcuts never the freeway

His failures suffer from a pitiful verticality

Separates the facts out with his feet

Loves only what fate and logic
    refuse to repay him

Dissolves in dilemmas the size
    of a fireball

His spirit has never had wings not even in dreams

His bread has no solution
    It is for public consumption

His speech is dog silence

Distances himself from the abyss toward the danger

Distances himself from the danger toward the abyss

His desperation can be seen from a bird's-eye view

Possesses what's taken away from him to hurl it at the beasts

Better restart his existence on the daily
    obliged to share it with himself

His endless letting his guard down

The storm splendor is his state of ecstasy

His truth broken like a reed
    or more like a well of dark water

Has the greatness of what drags along the ground

Corona de reyes

Una ciudad en la que el pánico adquiere la forma precisa de un tablero de ajedrez en donde las acciones suben y bajan axialmente por los costados de la montaña con vertientes de muslo de mujer y por los 4 horizontes que se disputan en una sala de juego

Se trata del paisaje habitual que cada quien ve como pájaro en jaula desde su ventana y que sólo puede ser fijado en los puños jamás en la mirada
Paisaje que no existe y del que se cae en cuenta a través del vidrio de un disparo y cuyos detritus miserables puestos a circular en las tarjetas postales reciben el bautismo en los acuarios Es el paisaje ideal que persiste en la memoria después que se han roto los muros de contención
Los himnos en la ablución de las alcantarillas celebran
las bodas de sus altos magistrados
siempre listo para hacer un mutis de conciencia
Paisaje que no se divisa nunca
Ciudad tabla rasa

Crown of Kings

A city where panic takes on the exact shape of a chessboard where stocks rise and fall axially up and down the mountainsides with gradients of woman thigh and down the 4 horizons under dispute in a cardroom

It is a common landscape seen by everyone from their windows like a bird in a cage and can only be fixed in fists never in a glance
Nonexistent landscape you fathom through the bullet-shattered glass and whose miserable detritus put to circulate in postcards are baptized in aquariums It is the ideal landscape lasting in memory after the walls of contention have been broken
The hymns in the sewer ablution celebrate
the wedding of their high magistrates
always ready to make a conscience exit
Landscape never caught sight of
City tabula rasa

Ases

El que mide palabras
y camina a saltos
se admira de ser como el rey náufrago
Devora palabras

El que juega a copas
por temor al rayo
no lleva metales
ni se refugia bajo árbol frondoso
Juega a copas

El que juega a espadas
tiende su vida
en la cuerda que lo ahoga
pronta como el rayo
Juega a espadas

El que juega a oros
sin súbditos ni superiores
anda dando gritos
    por la calle

Aces

The one who measures words
and walks in leaps
is admired for being like the castaway king
Devours words

The one who plays cups
out of fear of the lightning
doesn't wear metals
or hide beneath a leafy tree
Plays cups

The one who plays swords
lays life out
on the gallows rope
lightning fast
Plays swords

The one who plays coins
no subjects or superiors
walks the streets
   screaming

Legítima defensa

Mi seguridad termina
    puertas adentro del ojo del otro
Mi odio se diversifica como una red que tiene
    por eje el núcleo de la tormenta
No procedo más que en legítima defensa de lo que
    no soy
Se me permite situarme en un sitio estratégico
    de mi cuerpo para vigilarme mejor
Mis movimientos son tuyos ciudad
Me habitas cruelmente
Hostigas mi éxodo
Orientas mis pasos hacia los estados de postración
Armas mi equilibrio con frágiles varas
que el fuego alimenta

Legitimate Defense

My security ends
    behind the closed doors of the other's eye
My hate spreads like a net that has
    the storm nucleus for an axis
I do not press on more than in legitimate defense of what
    I am not
I am allowed to be located in a strategic place
    in my body to better watch over myself
My movements are yours city
You dwell in me cruelly
Batter my exodus
Direct my steps toward states of prostration
Arm my balance with fragile sticks
fed by fire

Tomas el pavimiento por la forma exacta de tu piel

Vives demasiado adentro y fuera de la ciudad
para poder cumplir a cabalidad tu oficio de vivir
Oficio que desempeñas del mejor modo en lugar
de otro y que te es impuesto desde dentro y de
fuera de ti mismo
para que de ningún modo puedas cumplirlo a
cabalidad

You Take Pavement as the Precise Shape of Your Skin

You live too inside and outside the city
to be able to fully achieve your profession of living
A profession you carry out in the best way instead
of another It is imposed on you from the inside and the
outside of you
so that you cannot in any way fully
achieve it

Las apuestas

No es el viento
lo que resiste en el ojo puesto sobre una flecha
Somos nosotros
Si arde una viga
    seguramente el incendio de tu casa
    no se aviene con la voluntad de vivir bien
Como los labios pegados contra el vidrio
    no desprenden el deseo la humedad del amor
Ni la víctima da importancia
    al hecho de andar descalza sobre las brasas
Clavar una mirada no significa
    cometer un crimen decir traición

Lo que una mordedura puede causar
    en un seno erecto
    no pone de pie a una audiencia vasta
Pides el silencio y obtienes la alarma general
Cuando duermes toda la ciudad
    despierta en tu sueño

The Wagers

It is not the wind
withstanding in the eye placed upon an arrow
It is us
If a beam burns
   your housefire surely
   does not get on with the will to live well
Like lips stuck to the glass
   do not sever the desire the wetness of love
Not even the victim gives importance
   to walking barefoot over the coals
To fix your gaze does not mean
   to commit a crime to declare treason

What a bite might cause
   in an erect breast
   does not bring a vast audience to its feet
You ask for silence and you get the general alarm
When you sleep the whole city
   wakes up in your dream

Arco de sílex

Cuanta piedra encuentres
    sobreponla a un esplendor
Besa la rama verde antes
    de que al fuego tierna baje
Una fuerza que puesta en acción
    no deja sangre en las manos
al ser disparado el arco de sílex
debería ser anulada bajo ruina y escombro

Y el mismo destino para lo que ofrece
    el seno que despunta con gloria
    semejante a un pequeño sol
En el roce del cuerpo que
    como mariposa se acerca demasiado al fuego
    para arder más rápido que el deseo

Así cuanto se pudre es aclimatación
    comparado con la fijeza del sueño
Cristales se rompen con sólo imaginar
    un gran salón desierto
Si entras en la mansedumbre por la boca del león
Vuelve
Resiste
Mas no de espaldas a ti mismo
    como quien sella su suerte
    con disparo a la sien
Empero emerge Agrégate a un despertar
Tal si tú mismo fueses la semilla salvaje

Arc of Silex

However much stone you find
    superimpose it on a splendor
Kiss the green branch before
    a force descends upon the tender fire
When it is put into action
    it leaves no blood on our hands
when the arc of silex is shot
the force must be voided beneath ruins and rubble

And the same destiny for what is offered by
    the breast rising with glory
    similar to a small sun
In the body brushing that
    like a butterfly gets too close to the fire
    to burn quicker than desire

So however much rots is acclimation
    compared to the dream fixedness
Glass breaks just thinking about
    a great room deserted
If you go into the docility through the lion's mouth
Come back
Resist
But don't turn your back on yourself
    like anyone who seals their fate
    with a shot to the temple
Despite it all show up Join the wakeup
As if you yourself were the wild seed

SISTEMA DE CONDUCTA

BEHAVIOR SYSTEM

Por partida doble

Hay algo dejado al azar y no es otra cosa que
la incógnita del juego cuyo control jamás
podrás asumir sin derramar la sangre del
contrario

Double Entry

There's something left to chance and it's nothing but
the mystery of the game whose control you will never
be able to take over without spilling the blood of
your rival

Jaula para occisos

En oír tierra cavernosa
   no hay clarividencia
En el ojo de la garza
   no hay clarividencia
Si suenas piedras
   el sonido tendrá exacta onda en el pozo
Si hay ahogado habrá
   espuma en los dientes

Si la mansedumbre es el polo opuesto
   de la daga en los dientes
Obtienes la cola de la serpiente
Si quemas óleos se incendia tu casa
Si vas al mercado vendes el cuerpo

Cage for the Slain

In hearing cavernous earth
   there is no clairvoyance
In the heron eye
   there is no clairvoyance
If you sound stones
   the noise will have the exact wave in the well
If someone drowns there will be
   foam on their teeth

If docility is the polar opposite
   of the dagger between teeth
You get the serpent's tail
If you burn oil paintings your house catches fire
If you go to the store you sell your body

Bestia I

Las riendas sueltas al punto de que la verdadera
marcha consiste en el más alto grado de paralización
    total

Bestia II

Al cabo descubres que el punto a donde te diriges
está demasiado cerca para darte cuenta que te
    confundes con él

Bestia III

La piel tirada en medio de
la vía rápida es la abstinencia

Beast I

Reins loose to the point that the actual
speed consists of the highest grade of total
    paralysis

Beast II

At last you figure out the place you are headed
is too close for you to realize you are
    mistaken for it

Beast III

The skin thrown in the middle of
the fast lane is abstinence

Suelo tomar extrañas determinaciones en ningún modo contrarias a mi
voluntad de ser libre pero que inexplicablemente están dirigidas contra mí
siempre de manera sistemática para anular cualquier
otra decisión que no sea la de permanecer
fijo en el muro de comienzo

I tend to make strange determinations that are in no way contradictory to
my will to be free but which are unexplainably directed against me
always in a systematic way in order to annul any
other decision that is not the decision to remain
stuck at the starting wall

Otra dirección

Comenzaste bien Pero una vez en camino
tus pasos toman otra dirección
Quieren sólo lo que la tierra espera de tu cuerpo
El laberinto fijo no la vía recta
El muro donde siempre se comienza
La inercia en lugar de la ruta
La posición horizontal
No el camino sino el descenso

A Different Direction

You started off okay But once on the road
your steps take a different direction
They only want what the earth expects from your body
The fixed maze not the straight stretch
The wall where it always begins
The inertia instead of the route
The horizontal position
Not the road but the descent

Órdenes

El terror es una orden general
La palabra es una orden general
Vivir o morir suponen estar siempre
atentos a una orden general

Orders

Terror is a general order
Word is a general order
To live or die supposes always being
aware of a general order

Imagen humeante

LAS MANOS A LA ESPALDA

BAJO EL CORRECTO NUDO

QUE EXUDA VISIONES

JUSTO AL NIVEL DEL CUELLO

QUE MUY TIESO SOBRE LA VENTANA

SE YERGUE FRENTE AL PANORAMA

(Y EL SUEÑO MUY ALTO)

Smoking Image

HANDS ON THE BACK

BENEATH THE CORRECT KNOT

WHICH EXUDES VISIONS

RIGHT AT THE NECK

WHICH QUITE STIFF ON THE WINDOW

RISES FACING THE PANORAMA

(AND THE VERY HIGH DREAM)

CARNET DE ENUMERACIONES

ENUMERATIONS CARD

Máscara de papel

Hay quienes me llaman por mi nombre
Hay quienes me llaman por omisión
Hay los que para conocerme
    se dirigen a los poderes públicos
Son tres
Y tres las potencias divinas que
    al hablarme dicen
Toda noche arroja una oveja ciega
    sobre la tinta de las pesadillas
Imagen de una sola cara
    que comparto con un ángel milenario
Así que sueño soy manso de carácter
Irascible tan pronto me desdoblo
    en dos en tres en cuatro partes
        iguales siempre a mí mismo
A decir verdad
Requiero una palabra que hable en lugar de mi boca
Un traje que llene el vacío de mi cuerpo
Un duende que haga mis veces
En vez de tierra un pedestal de cartón
Un haz de trébol en lugar de una espada
Cuando necesito darme a conocer
    pongo un escalpelo
    en las manos de mi interlocutor

Paper Mask

There are people who call me by my name
Others who name me by omission
There are those who address the public
   authorities in order to know me
There are three
And three the divine powers
   when they speak to me they say
Each night hurls a blind sheep
   over nightmare ink
Image of a lone face
   I share with a millennial angel
So I dream I am docile
Irritable as soon as I unfold
   in two in three in four parts
     always the same as me
To tell the truth
I require a word to speak in place of my mouth
A suit to fill the emptiness of my body
A duende to stand in for me
Instead of earth a cardboard pedestal
An ace of spades instead of a sword
When I need to make myself known
   I place a scalpel
   in the hands of my interlocutor

Cubrir la duda con un mantel de fiesta

Sustituir el brazo por un artefacto
    que se le parece

Presionar un revólver contra algo blando
   con tal de romper el silencio

Vadear el hilo de la conversación
    más allá del diálogo que se
      interrumpe con la rapidez
     de una descarga eléctrica

Aproximarse al sismo en sentido inverso
    al deseo de huir
 y en el preciso momento
    en que se le oye venir

Pisar en terreno falso con pie de plomo
Hacer de la liebre una máscara de león
Sumar distancias ajenas al viaje
    que no se realiza

Poner un reguero de pólvora
   en el centro de una pista de baile

Crecer en la hierba siempre hacia abajo

Cruzarse de brazos para precipitar
    el autoestrangulamiento

Leer en la página en blanco lo que
    aún no se ha escrito ni se escribirá nunca

Cubrir la duda con un mantel de fiesta
    que da a la casa extraña
      apariencia de templo

Oponer escudos de hojas a la fuerza del huracán
es prueba de confianza no en el brazo
sino en la fuerza del huracán

To Cover Doubt with a Fancy Tablecloth

To substitute the arm for a similar
    artifact

To shoot the revolver against something soft
  as long as silence is broken

To ford the line of conversation
  beyond the dialogue
    interrupted by the quickness
    of an electrical charge

To grow closer to the earthquake in the opposite direction
    of the desire to flee
  and at the exact moment
    when you hear it coming

To step on unstable ground with a lead foot
Make the hare a lion's mask
Add distances far from the journey
    not taken

To place a trail of gunpowder
  in the middle of a dance floor

To always grow in the grass downward

To cross your arms in anticipation of
    self-strangulation

To read on the blank page what is
  still unwritten and won't ever be

To cover doubt with a fancy tablecloth
  which gives the house a strange
    appearance of temple

To place a shield made of leaves against hurricane force
is a vote of confidence not for the arm
but for the hurricane force

Ciudado frágil

La torsión del azar
pide el cuello de cisne frágil
de cristal
de agua de fuente
de ciudadano común
de victimario
de fuego de extrema unción
de piedra posesa
de tinta de calamar
de sangre
de mandamiento
de noche
de nada

Warning Fragile

The twisting of fate
requires the neck of a fragile swan made
of glass
of fountain water
of common citizen
of killer
of extremely devoted fire
of possessed stone
of squid ink
of blood
of commandment
of night
of nothing

La mirada quiere claraboyas a ras de la conciencia
El odio la pelambre del animal razonable
Agarrarse a las manos del contrario
    en lo más miserable de la batalla
La mano del huracán postigos para dar la voz de
    alarma
El amor criptas de acondicionamiento
    para meter dos cuerpos en uno
La palabra la garganta de los grandes valles
La clarividencia el instrumento para abrir
    el órgano de la visión
La duda el oxígeno de los incendios

The glance wants skylights level with consciousness
The hate the reasonable animal pelts
To grab hold of the hands of the rival
    in the most miserable part of battle
The hurricane hand posterns to sound the voice of
    alarm
The love crypts of reconditioning
    to stick two bodies in one
The word the throat from the great valleys
The clairvoyance the instrument to open
    the vision organ
The doubt the oxygen of fires

Fuerza bruta

A fuerza de apretar se adquiere el hábito
    de hacer prisioneros
Se adquiere el hábito de entrar en guerra
A fuerza de vivir los ángeles se doblegan
El grito es el reverso de lo que el silencio reprime
    bajo tu piel
La mano envuelve
Las lágrimas depositan sal en las alcantarillas
El tacto aproxima pero el deseo aleja
Condena
La piedra elude toda consideración
    hacia las flores
    que saltan como pájaro en mano
Imposible vivir en dos cuerpos a la vez
    conservando un espíritu ameno
El silencio sabe renovar el olvido
Una sola voz no vale por un puño
A viva fuerza
Señor

Brute Force

By dint of squeezing one acquires the habit
   of making prisoners
Acquires the habit of going to war
By dint of living the angels are vanquished
The scream is the opposite of what silence represses
   under your skin
The hand surrounds
The tears amass salt in the sewers
The touch brings closer but the desire moves away
Condemns
The stone avoids any consideration
   of flowers
   hopping like a bird in hand
Impossible to live in two bodies at once
   maintaining a pleasant disposition
The silence knows how to renew forgetfulness
Just one voice isn't worth a fist
Forcibly
Sir

Salud
Escritorio público para llevar bajo el brazo
como un portafolio del que no haremos una tumba
Situado en la vía pública
    es la alfombra tomada por asalto
En un terreno yermo forma la depresión
    en que se ha hundido la iglesia
En el palacio es pila bautismal para armas blancas
En el mercado exorcismo que pronunciamos en vano
Lavatorio en nada parecido a un esponsal
celebrado en el último piso del edificio
    que se derrumba
Río cuya lengua arrastra nuestros nombres
    hacia el desastre que no puede ser evitado
No sabiendo a dónde dirigirme
    ni dónde descansar
Escritorio público para llevar bajo el brazo
Soportable tumba
Salud

To your health
Public desk meant to carry under your arm
like a briefcase we won't turn into a grave
Located on the freeway
     it is the carpet taken by storm
In a wasteland a hollow forms
     from a sinking church
In the palace it is a baptismal font for bladed weapons
In the market an exorcism we utter in vain
Washroom not even close to a betrothal
celebrated on the top floor of the building
     in ruins
River whose tongue drags our names
     toward the unavoidable disaster
Me not knowing where to turn
     or where to rest
Public desk meant to carry under your arm
Bearable grave
To your health

La contrariedad nacida de oírme
    continuamente a mí mismo
pone al descubierto una gran queja
formulada a todo lo largo de mi cuerpo
Cuerpo innoble o tejido de palabras acéfalo
en uno de cuyos extremos se agitan nubes de tormenta
Herida cuyas hebras aprisionan
raíces puños nervios sexos
    ciudades enteras
que pudren sus lomos desnudos
        en la quijada de la ola
La forma discontinua sistemática en que mis pasos
una vez dados trazan el surco profundo
        donde se me incrusta
    es la situación inversa
        de todo despertar
Sonido de pluma que no deja marca viva
    en la roca Rendición extrema
        Golpe

The opposition born from constantly
   hearing myself
reveals a great complaint
formulated along the full length of my body
Evil body or acephalous word tissue
storm clouds stir at one end of it
Wound whose strands imprison
roots fists nerves sexes
   entire cities
their naked spines rotting
      in the jaw of the wave
The systematic sporadic way in which my steps
once taken trace the deep groove
      where I am embedded
   it is the opposite circumstance
      of total awakening
Feather sound that leaves no living mark
   on the rock Surrender extreme
      Blow

ABISMO PÚBLICO

PUBLIC ABYSS

Hábitos

De niño adquirí el hábito de arrastrar los pies Inclinación un tanto
monstruosa que pronto se apoderó de todo mi ser
Se trata de la vía de aprendizaje para llegar a ser un ofidio
En consecuencia mis amigos si tienen que hablarme deben asegurarse de
que estoy en algún lado
Tarde o temprano volverás a tu primer estado
¿Súplica o enfermedad? Resígnate
Dicho esto se protegen contra la mordedura de culebra
El cuerpo sabe adaptarse siempre a las condiciones del suelo
La piel forma valles y cordilleras que se trasladan como una onda fija
aparentemente sin que nada se mueva
El movimiento de las patas es alterno de dos en dos ellas obedecen al
cuerpo sin dilación se diría que de un modo mecánico ¿Cómo regresar?
Esa es la cuestión
puesto que la dificultad se erige en absurdo se petrifica en la marcha del
órgano que repta Todo el mal reside en haber comenzado un nuevo cuerpo
demasiado tarde demasiado tarde

Habits

As a kid I picked up the habit of dragging my feet A somewhat monstruous inclination that soon took over my entire being

It's the way I learned to become an ophidian

As a result my friends if they must speak to me should ensure that I am somewhere

Sooner or later you will return to your first state

Plea or sickness? Give up

Having said this they are protected against the snakebite

The body always knows how to adapt to the conditions on the ground

The skin forms valleys and mountain ranges that relocate like a fixed wave seemingly immobile

The movement of the legs alternates two by two they quickly obey the body you could say mechanically How to return?

That is the question

since the difficulty of it becomes absurd it is petrified in the march of the crawling organ All evil lies in having begun a new body too late too late

Dentro de la roca vacía

Suponte que llegas a ese sitio donde no te han llamado
precisamente cuando menos lo deseabas de tus pasos
que sin vacilación
te han llevado a tan extraño lugar
Imagínate ahora la sala vacía
    donde se prepara una ceremonia de la que
llegado el momento dejas de ser testigo para convertirte en actor
Como si te faltara aliento
y cayeras hacia el centro anulado por una enorme
    fuerza de atracción
—Es tarde Regresa

Inside the Empty Rock

Suppose you get to that point where they haven't called you
right when you least wanted it from your steps
that have confidently
taken you to such a strange place
Now imagine the empty room
  where a ceremony is being prepared
when the time comes you are no longer a witness but an actor
As if you were out of breath
and you were falling toward the center canceled by an enormous
  force of attraction
—It's late Turn back

De los reos

Imaginemos a un enfermo de muerte que ha estado soñando la condición
para que siga vivo es la de que continúe soñando
Si el soñador es por caso un artista ciertamente elegirá un prado hermoso
cruzado por un río que no ha visto antes en cuyas aguas apacibles sumerge
su cuerpo

Si actor convengamos en las excelencias de su nuevo papel remitiéndonos
a un ejercicio brillante digno del teatro Noh

Mas por tranquilo que se encuentre el soñador la insatisfacción entra por
su ojo medio abierto que le permite aún divagar

Momentáneamente él querrá ser otra cosa Un árbol un pájaro un largo
sonido en la noche Y este deseo será más fuerte que el recuerdo de sus
momentos más dichosos

Algunas veces en un esfuerzo final abre sus ojos más allá de lo que les está
permitido a los párpados y entonces pronuncia esas palabras mágicas
(aprendidas en los libros) que dan a las sábanas un color viscoso He allí la
justa advertencia de que ni siquiera en la urna se sentirá bastante tranquilo

On Prisoners

Let's imagine someone deathly ill who has been dreaming the one condition to stay alive is that he keep dreaming
If the dreamer in this case is an artist he will certainly choose a beautiful meadow traversed by a river he's never seen in whose peaceful waters he submerges his body

If he's an actor let's agree upon the excellence of his new role referring to a brilliant rehearsal worthy of Noh theater

Yet as calm as the dreamer is dissatisfaction arrives through his half-opened eye which still allows him to digress

Momentarily he will want to be something else A tree a bird a long night sound And this desire will be stronger than the memory of his most fortunate moments

Sometimes in a final act of strength he opens his eyes beyond what his eyelids are allowed and then he pronounces these magical words (learned from books) that give the sheets a viscous color Here then is the just warning that not even in the urn is one able to find peace

Sentencia

Generalmente el veneno que doy a los perros
para extinguir su raza maldita me suele ser
devuelto en forma de calculadas raciones
que mis jefes superiores a la vista de todos
se empeñan con éxito en darme a beber
Reírse no mejorará la situación
Fijarse al banco
Hazlo con toda calma dispones de cinco segundos
Sólo para probar
Complace a tus padres

Sentence

Generally the poison I give the dogs
to wipe out their wretched race tends to be
given back to me in the form of calculated rations
which my bosses in view of everyone
successfully insist on giving me to drink
Laughing won't make the situation any better
To be fastened to the bench
Do it calmly you've got five seconds
Just for fun
Make your parents happy

Mandamiento

Desde ahora mismo
el difunto debe hacerse la idea de que la postura horizontal es en resumidas
cuentas la más cómoda Este pensamiento será fijado a su cuerpo para que
le sirva de bastón y pueda con él restablecer el equilibrio perdido y ponerse
súbitamente de pie a fin de que vuelva por sus pasos señor a darse justicia

Commandment

From now on
the dead must make up their minds that the horizontal position is in short
the most comfortable This idea will be fixed to their bodies so that it acts
as a cane and as such lost balance will be regained and they will suddenly
stand up with the goal of returning with these steps reader to claim justice

C14

La proliferación de estos espectros para
esparcimiento de magistrados banales
que penden de sus altos salarios
y de las buenas tardes
como la araña del
techo carcomido
Se está bien
allá arriba
señal del
C14

C14

The proliferation of these specters for the
amusement of banal magistrates who
hang from their high salaries
and the good evenings
like the spider on the
wormeaten ceiling
It is okay up
there sign
al from
C14

UN OJO DE CONTRAPESO

AN EYE AS COUNTERWEIGHT

Piedra sobre piedra

El diálogo no se construye
como una gradería por cuyos peldaños
han de desplazarse rápidamente
los vivos corriendo hacia los muertos

Por el contrario
es una muralla siempre levantada
entre la palabra y el gesto
donde todo ademán cuesta sostenerse
en el vacío que se forma en medio de los cuerpos
de los vivos corriendo hacia los muertos

Hecha no de vocablos heroicos tiernas
promesas de amante sino de alaridos
de puntas de lanzas en las almenas
cuyas paredes sangran por ambos costados
No de adobes sino de
    alambre de exterminio en masa
de vómito
    de persecución de rótulos de huesos
y falsos esqueletos de vivos
corriendo hacia los muertos

Stone upon Stone

Dialogue is not built
like a grandstand whose steps
must be traveled quickly by
the living running toward the dead

On the contrary
it is a wall always raised
between word and gesture
where any motion is hard to hold
in the emptiness forming amid the bodies
of the living running toward the dead

Made not of heroic words a lover's
tender promises but howls
of spearheads in the battlements
whose walls bleed out from both sides
Not adobe but
    barbed wire of extermination en masse
vomit
    tagged bone persecution
and fake skeletons of the living
running toward the dead

Sumiso
Para dar seguridad
mi ojo tiene por espejo una vitrina de redimir
Sólo así acepta la idea de ineptitud
que se le obliga a soportar
muy rígida en el cuerpo que le sirve
de punto de apoyo y a través del cual
el ojo desciende y gira sin poder
hacer otra cosa que mirar
Sumiso

Submissive
For safety's sake
my eye has a payoff shop window for a mirror
This is the only way it accepts the idea of ineptitude
which it is obliged to put up with
the idea is quite rigid in my body which serves
as a support point and down it
the eye descends and spins powerless
to do anything else but watch
Submissive

De una caja de asfódelos empujada contra la corriente devengas la pérdida de tiempo De un cuerpo roto a pedazos en el instante vacío de la tierra donde desaparece se recuerda no la ceremonia sino el cuchillo No las flores sino el rostro del convencido Con algas en la mano se obtiene sólo la piedra de río Mirando el cielo a través de los árboles no encuentras los frutos perdidos en el suelo ni el pez ni la certeza ni el día

From a box of asphodels pushed against the current you earn the loss of time From a body broken to pieces at the empty instant of the earth where it disappears what is recalled is not the ceremony but the knife Not the flowers but the face of the committed With seaweed in hand you only get the riverstone Watching the sky through the trees you don't find the fruit lost on the ground or the fish or the certainty or the day

Pon atención Date cuenta Concéntrate El milagro vendrá Es posible que venga Sucede que las condiciones para un sismo siempre están dadas Espera la orden Sólo falta el día la hora el instante fatal Apretar el botón Bajar la guardia Caer de bruces en prueba de haber estado en pie la mitad en el fuego la mitad en el fango Dotar a la tierra de tus propios estados de condensación Hay dilaciones oportunas Hay tiempo de sobra Hay mares que son de piedra Pedestales que se inclinan Remoción de hierbas Una botella inmersa no es un estado de conciencia has oído Lleva tu mal a cuestas Empújalo tras de ti hacia el fondo del barranco pues la rigidez no hará de la piedra vulgar una mesa de comer de vivir una mesa de dormir

Pay attention Realize Focus The miracle is coming It might come It so happens that conditions for an earthquake are always given Wait for the order What is missing Only the day the hour the fatal instant To push the button To let your guard down To fall flat on your face to prove you've been on your feet half in fire half in mud To equip the earth with your own states of condensation There are opportune delays There is more than enough time There are stone seas Pedestals inclining Removal of weeds An immersed bottle is not a state of consciousness you have heard Carry your evil upon your shoulders Get it behind you down toward the bottom of the ravine since the rigidness will not make of the vulgar stone a dining table a living table a sleeping table

La quinta parte del espíritu es el deseo de huir

Cuando se pronuncian ciertas palabras existe el peligro visible de que la mitad del espíritu huya del cuerpo Otra parte no puede ser desprendida Es allí donde comienza la vida en común Se trata de hacer lo posible para que retorne al sitio de origen Halar el espíritu atraerlo con el brillo de los imanes Convencerlo requiere un esfuerzo de paciencia digno de cíclopes Es la oblación cuando ocurre una desgracia La quinta parte del espíritu es el deseo de huir Otra ha sido fijada a los ganchos de reses Tocas madera y desaparece Otra parte perfectamente visible jamás ha existido Otra lucha contra circunstancias adversas Una parte del cuerpo se olvida que existe la otra parte del cuerpo
Comienza a halar hacia su lado

The Fifth Part of the Spirit Is the Desire to Flee

When certain words are uttered there is the visible danger of half the spirit fleeing the body The other part won't come off That's where life in common starts It is about trying as much as possible to return to the site of origin Pull the spirit attract it with the shiny magnets Convincing it requires a patience worthy of cyclopes It is a sacrifice when something bad happens The fifth part of the spirit is the desire to flee Another part has been hung on meat hooks You knock on wood and it disappears Another part perfectly visible never existed Another struggles against adverse circumstances Another part of the body forgets that another part of the body exists
It starts to pull toward its side

Entre jaulas de occisos cuya proximidad se oye a varias leguas de distancia
como una palabra demasiado espesa o un túnel difícil de atravesar
    quien desee vivir elija
    un pequeño estertor
y utilizando su garganta como instrumento para disparar
láncelo
antes de que sea tarde
Anuncio que debe leerse Párate
O grito recién nacido de una boca
    que gira en las manivelas
Sonámbulo
    En los pestillos en los pedales de freno
y al que el muro presta una pantalla fija
    como túnica de alumbrar

Entre jaulas de fieras
la fortuna consiste en pasearse del lado afuera
en medio de árboles que saludan
desde sus ramas
El porte el paso diestro la mano en el pecho la descripción del gesto la
facultad de saber hablar en público el ojo saludable la soberbia el ojal el
traje negro el doblez bien hecho
qué ventajas dan sobre el resto
Sentado en el banquillo
acariciar el lomo del animal
Ciudad selva de huir

Among the cages of the slain whose proximity you can hear from various
leagues of distance like a word that's too thick or a tunnel that's difficult to
cross
      whoever wants to live choose
      a small death rattle
and using your throat as an instrument to discharge
throw it
before it's too late
A warning that ought to be read Stand up
Or cry newly born from a mouth
   spinning in the handles
Sleepwalker
   In the latches in the brake pedals
and to whom the wall lends a fixed screen
   like an illuminating tunic

Among the cages of the beasts
fortune consists of strolling along the outer side
amid trees greeting
from their branches
The appearance the skilled stride the hand on a chest the description of a
gesture the ability to know how to speak in public the healthy eye the pride
the buttonhole the black suit the well-ironed crease
what advantages they have over the rest
Sitting on a bench
to pet the animal's back
City fleeing jungle

Appendix

An Interview with Juan Calzadilla

Víctor Rodríguez Núñez

Translated by Katherine M. Hedeen and Olivia Lott

This interview was originally published in the Colombian literary magazine *Revista Universidad Cooperativa de Colombia*, in 1995. A later, definitive version appeared in *La poesía sirve para todo*, published in Havana, Cuba (Ediciones Unión, 2008).

I met him on Caracas Street; not in the capital of Venezuela, HIS city (he is, after all, its most characteristic poet), but in Medellín, Colombia's dreary downtown, which doesn't have much to do with poetry at all. And beneath a sun that could snap your soul in two.

We were both walking along the same sidewalk, but in opposite directions. I carelessly approached, like one ought to with someone who has dared to confess: "At my funeral I was talking bad about myself / and I died laughing."

In a world where it is increasingly rare to find intelligence, humor, warmth, and poetry, Juan Calzadilla has a lot to offer: simple, uncomplicated, and with a vast amount of work to his name.

We immediately began this conversation. I sincerely hoped it would never end (and I still do). In less than five minutes we became accomplices, planning certain noble crimes. I'm convinced we knew each other in some other life, either past or future.

Though he was born (in 1931) in a small town called Altagracia de Orituco, with his birth a new chapter of magic realism didn't begin. Juan is undoubtedly the poet of the city, the peasant not from Paris but from Caracas . . . The street in Medellín where we met?

211

> Citizen of an enchanted forest, as soon as I entered it I discovered I was
> a city peasant.

For me, writing poetry wasn't a choice; it was the result of a natural process. You try your hand at it from the time you're young and, somehow, you keep at it, and eventually you're just driven to do it. The choice happens after you realize you're good at it, and that only becomes a reality by doing it. Ultimately, it's an expressive need. As a poet I began at twenty-three, just out of high school, writing something similar to Spanish poetry. That was when I discovered a new universe. I come from the opposition, from the political opposition that took place in Venezuela at the end of the 1950s. I began writing in a remote town in the province, during breaks from the political struggle against [Marcos] Pérez Jiménez. Since I had to spend a lot of time in seclusion, I read a lot. Out of that time, and inspired by reading the Spanish classics, came a great need to express myself. I wrote a book and sent it off to a contest in Caracas organized by the World Peace Festival. I won the prize, which consisted of a trip to Moscow. That's when I became committed to a literary destiny, which immediately branched out. On the one hand, research and art criticism, which is how I've earned my living. On the other, poetry.

> We exist because of the similarity we maintain with ourselves at each
> moment. That is why, more than singular, we are simply obvious. To
> exist is the most palpable proof that we repeat ourselves.

Every Latin American poet has two basic nutrients. The first is our own tradition, our world, and the second is a foreign, international influence. It's impossible for a poet to not have both or to depend exclusively on just one. Within the national framework, in what surrounded us, there were two poets who served as an example: Vicente Gerbasi and Rodolfo Moleiros. The latter is not well known, but he was a very rigorous poet, a student of poetry, and, above all, very communicative. He wrote metered poetry, within the tradition but with a modern edge. In other words, a minor poet who greatly stimulated us to create, who represented a lot for the youth from the era of the dictatorship. In a way, he opened our eyes to the need for rigor, to do things with continuity. Internationally, there was some

wavering, something like two phases: first, Spanish literature, the classic models that you learn about at the university, the first influences you have; second, the poets of the Renaissance and then others closer to us in time. My *Primeros poemas* were written in rhyme. That all happened before there was a kind of rupturing, the presence of other elements that influenced our generation.

Poetry is a branch of grammar from which flowers bloom.

I firmly believe in the possibility of learning poetry. It is something that we can consider, above all, as the acquisition of language skills. This doesn't mean that I think someone is going to become a poet because they study how to do it, not at all. The main thing here is an expressive need; that there is this vocation struggling to manifest itself, a restlessness that you sometimes feel. In other words, the urgency to use words to say something that, when you're young, is extremely vague, but then later takes shape. So, there are two moments: the first is learning and the second is vocation. I think a poet emerges, fundamentally, from the exercise of prose. A poet who does not practice writing prose, who does not use it on a daily basis, rarely comes to have a knowledge of language, THE fundamental tool for poetry. In my case, the first thing I learned was to make a living by writing journalism. I developed good skills from prose, and that has facilitated my access to poetry. Even now, I return to prose to rediscover myself in poetry.

What makes a right-winger a right-winger is that they think and act like a right-winger. What makes a left-winger a left-winger is that they limit themselves exclusively to thinking like a left-winger.

I am part of the so-called Generation of the 1960s. In one way, it's a term that does not define what happened in our poetry from those decisive years. You can't really say there was a movement, a coherent grouping like there have been at other historical moments. I think I definitely belong to a generation that is characterized by having a clear commitment. Of course, it's important to be "generation conscious." A generation is the concrete way in which an ideology manifests itself; in our case, challenging the system and certain established literary values. In our generation there

are poets of great influence, of great strength. They revealed themselves in a double sense: one, by responding to what was happening in terms of poetic values, and another, by taking an ethical position in the face of the political situation we were experiencing at the time. For most of us, it was a necessity to fight and to be committed, even to the point of taking up arms. This kind of situation, which forces the poet to face confrontation, was a response to very particular circumstances. That historical moment, which had an impact on poetry and which has not happened again, is what distinguishes us. The poets that came later, in the 1970s, are characterized by the almost total dissolution of that kind of ideology.

> My generation's taste for violence. But not so much for violence itself
> as for violent words. You could see them walking in the middle of
> traffic.

I don't know why there's so much talk about groups; they are almost always just a myth. The group Tabla Redonda [Round Table] was a guild that held certain opinions about poetry and society. I belonged to what was called El Techo de la Ballena [The Roof of the Whale], which was politically committed but which ultimately, in properly poetic language, sought great freedom. We liked to confront violence in an un-propagandistic way; we were dissidents of Marxist dogmatism. As for Tabla Redonda, they followed the political guidelines of the official left. There was a big difference between our poetry and theirs; what we did was not in keeping with orthodoxy. Today I don't distinguish between the poets of these two groups because things change and those changes lead to different criteria. I cannot say that we were the good guys and they were the bad guys because in both groups there were interesting poets. In Tabla Redonda there was Rafael Cadenas, who was well known and who has later written poetry that has nothing to do with his initial positions, with his group's agenda. Also, Arnaldo Acosta Bello. And in El Techo de la Ballena there was Efraín Hurtado, who was a lightning flash in those first moments. Poets can embody, in many ways, the libertarian attitude.

> How easy to be a poet when you think it's right to attribute more sense
> to words than to things!

I don't believe poetry is destined to become a means to an end. I think this aesthetic of art as a goal in itself is generally related to decadence. Poetry has taken a turn; it has changed a lot since the 1960s. Today poetry leans toward the urban, to the use of common vocabulary, to go directly to the point. Obviously, this is going to give it a nonformal nature and the concept of its autonomy is lost. I don't agree with [William Carlos] Williams that the function of poetry is to reveal. I admire him because he was one of those who envisioned a new field for poetry: that of everyday things. More than to reveal, the function of poetry is to transcend the language with which everyday things are expressed. The concept of revelation is metaphysical and therefore more reclusive than you might think. I don't agree with Matisse either, that every creative effort is interior, that a work of art is not authentic if it is not made by interiority. To think in those terms is to accept that there is a specific language for poetry that is not valid for everything else. Everyone has their own way—through internalization, through experience—of dealing with language. But you can't talk about poetry without externalization.

You don't need to put it forward to yourself. You just have to want it.

Poe claimed to be able to detail, step by step, the process by which he created a text. More or less the same thing happens to me. The poetry of our times is characterized by having become highly self-aware. Even the process of how it gestates has become something more important than the actual result. Yes, poetry is deeply, sincerely self-critical. I see myself in this way of defining poetry, presenting it as an open work. An open work not in the sense of conclusive but as a loophole to go in and out of, to question oneself. This is why I am very distanced from the model that prevails in my country, this idea of the poem as an autonomous reality. There is an open poetry and a closed one, and today's poetry must be open. In other words, permanently questioning its formulation, constantly falling into contradiction and breaking with style. I tend to consider poetry as an immediate experience for understanding reality. A poetry based on the everyday, on what happens around me, on what I read. A poetry that takes as its base what others have said and eliminates all metaphysical pretensions.

The glow of the concept behind the words. And this sometimes, when
they are capable of blooming. In any season.

I repeat, I am not fond of Williams's thesis about the poem as a mechanical
artifact made with words and destined to convey an idea, a feeling. That is
the line of poetry that they tried to instill in us when I was young and now
it's gaining momentum in Venezuela again. This has always been consid-
ered as the ultimate solution for poetry, that form prevails and meaning is
exhausted. It is what has come to be called visual, concretist poetry. I declare
myself an enemy of considering poetry an object in itself. The principle of
modernity is in the use of mediums provided by technology. Television or
photography can be used for poetry, but they do not replace it. In other
words, poetry is a genre that does not progress. Nor do I believe that the
poet, as Baudelaire argued, loses strength when he pursues a moral goal.
Breton didn't think Baudelaire was a surrealist because he saw in him too
religious a conscience. Baudelaire said his prayers every day. Who was he
praying to? It doesn't matter if it was to God or to the devil, he still prayed.

I don't write about what goes through my head. I write about what my
head goes through.

Inspiration is daily work, our ability to concentrate on our work. It is not
something that comes suddenly; it is built like the poem itself. As for orig-
inality, it's a term that is highly questioned; today hardly anyone looks for
it. We have great freedom to engage with and use an abundance of resources
from the present and the past. And perfection doesn't exist either. Some-
one said that whatever is considered perfect cannot be achieved, that every-
thing is by nature imperfect. You have written a poem and, once finished,
you can change it, correct it. I believe in perfection only as an effort to
reach a poem that is as clean as it can be, the harmony between form and
meaning, the word that surrounds what you want to say, in its parts and
in its entirety. The perfect thing is when you agree with what you have
achieved, the synchronization between form and meaning. It happens that
in contemporary poetry form is being imposed, gradually displacing con-
tent, imposing the grammatical structure as the nucleus. But I lean more
toward meaning than toward form.

> The consumers and possible users of poetry have been informed of the risks they are exposed to, given the fact that, after a certain amount of time, they may end up realizing that this product was never fashionable.

I think poetry today has the same presence and diffusion as it had before. Unless you're talking about before World War II, when poetry had a much greater public presence and poets fulfilled a social function. Poetry was conceived of then as a means of communication; its purpose was the same as when it was oral expression. Obviously, we do not currently have the great poets of fifty years ago. This is offset by the richness and diversity of today's poetry. There is a crisis in poetry these days because it has become more multifaceted; it has multiplied. And poets have gotten more skeptical in terms of changing reality; they refuse to present themselves as optimistic. In this crisis, poetry tries to find a lifeline by reflecting on itself. Of course, everything can be said with poetry, either with encoded poetry or with direct poetry. I have written in other literary genres; I have written narrative essays but without much success. I have a surrealist novel from 1973, called *Bicéfalo*. Poetry is a record of the intellection of the world; it is a form of knowledge and, if it doesn't show up as a verbal synthesis, it still shows up.

> Those who look at themselves in a mirror are only there because they look at themselves.

The fact that I'm also a visual artist has not distanced me from poetry; quite the contrary. As I already said, writing prose has helped me as a poet. Prose is an improvement tool; it helps you to analyze things with words, which poetry doesn't easily give you. The latter is a preassembled genre, where reflection occurs later. If you achieve a mastery of prose, writing poetry will be much easier. The other thing is that I am a very visual subject, and I express it through painting, calligraphy as a way of assembling the text, and in another way through images. It should be noted that the visual is an ingredient of poetry. So that poetry and painting are concomitant; they are two languages that come from the same stalk. Why do sad poems predominate over happy ones? Because we are living in a time of readjustment of all the forces, a time of great skepticism. Pessimism is reflected

above all when dealing with the social. Lately, poetry has lost that function. Now it mostly concerns the existential condition of the poet, as a helpless being who feels the tearing of language. What we are experiencing today on a global scale is calamitous. But there is no denying that this gives poets a great stimulus to carry out their work.

> Consider me a wild man, sirs, but with enough intelligence to not
> pretend I'm not. Oh, I don't need to modernize!

The social changes carried out by the government of Hugo Chávez have been very positive and are modifying the behavior, the idiosyncrasies, and the way of thinking of Venezuelans, championing confidence and self-respect and consequently the participation and leadership of the common people. Today, in every social sphere, Venezuela is a kind of great political melting pot, a laboratory, a country that is rapidly transforming, to the point that it has led people to believe that the socialist model can pass from a utopia to a concrete reality, becoming an example to follow for other Latin Americans. The radical nature of the changes that are taking place has, of course, affected the intellectual world and the cultural scene. These changes manifest themselves with equal parts acrimony and radicalism in the fields of art and literature, in such a way that they have led to the division of the country, also in culture, into two intransigent blocs. On the one hand, those of us who support the process and, in some way, identify with it and, on the other, those who defend the cultural project of previous governments, a project (if one can speak of such) characterized by the exclusion of the masses. I do not want to say that we are divided into left-wing and right-wing intellectuals, since many of those who oppose Chávez's revolution were members of left-wing parties until recently, and even call themselves leftists who "dissent from the tyrant's principles."

> How to not be what I am
> How to not be what I was.

It's significant that the rejection of Chávez's policies by this right-wing (or not) intelligentsia begins with a critique of populism and happens side by side with the greatest contempt for and rejection of the popular measures

undertaken by the state. In literary matters, multiple reading support networks have been created and massive editorial plans have been put into practice that favor a large number of people who previously had no access to any means of publication. Something similar is happening in education, with the missions created to teach reading or train professionals as an alternative to the closed autonomous university system. Despite the political conflict and the consequent delimitation of the intellectual field, the two blocs have recently come closer together, approximations generated by a more comprehensive and less mediated (in the best sense) reading of state policies. At the same time, supported by the climate of peace and existing freedoms, a new left-wing intelligentsia is emerging, formed in the heat of the missions and in the incentives for creative writing that have spread like a rhizome throughout the country, creating a fever for knowledge that, sooner or later, if the process is not interrupted by foreign intervention, could result in our having a highly civilized society, one that we promoted unsuccessfully in the days of El Techo de la Ballena and the urban guerrilla.

Here lies the one who thought he could free himself from this trance too.

Acknowledgments

The translators would like to thank the editors of the following literary journals, where earlier versions of some of these poems first appeared: *Asymptote* ("i live day by day," "i see me," "hitting the abyss," "with bad manners," and "the magma must return"), *Circumference* ("a civil servant celebrates a ritual," "waiting for salvation," and "urinal"), and *Fence* ("Pay attention . . ." and "Among the cages of the slain . . .").

Additional thanks to Forrest Gander for his thoughtful and generous reading of our work; to Wisconsin Poetry Series editors Jesse Lee Kercheval and Sean Bishop for their championing of poetry and translation; to Dennis Lloyd and the entire staff of the University of Wisconsin Press for their support; to Víctor Rodríguez Núñez for introducing us to Calzadilla's poetry and for all he has done behind the scenes to make this project a reality; and to the community who supports poetry in translation, especially Don Mee Choi, Paul Cunningham, Kristin Dykstra, Michelle Gil-Montero, Johannes Göransson, Steve Halle, Ignacio Infante, Joyelle McSweeney, and Jeannine Pitas.

Juan Calzadilla is one of Venezuela's most celebrated poets, painters, and art critics. He is the author of more than twenty books of poetry and, in 1996, was awarded Venezuela's National Visual Arts Prize. His work, across both mediums, is characterized by political consciousness and formal innovation; prominent images include the surrealist chaos of urban space, the violent

dehumanization of uneven modernity, and the abject probing of social and aesthetic status quos. In 1961, he cofounded the radical neo-avant-garde collective El Techo de la Ballena (The Roof of the Whale).

Katherine M. Hedeen is a prize-winning translator of poetry and an essayist. A specialist in Latin American poetry, she has translated some of the most respected voices from the region into English. Her latest book-length publications include *prepoems in postspanish* by Jorgenrique Adoum, *Book of the Cold* by Antonio Gamoneda, *Every Beat Is Secret* by Fina García Marruz, *Almost Obscene* by Raúl Gómez Jattin, and *rebel matter* by Víctor Rodríguez Núñez. She is the

coeditor, with Welsh poet Zoë Skoulding, of the groundbreaking transatlantic translation anthology *Poetry's Geographies*. Her work has been a finalist for both the Best Translated Book Award and the National Translation Award. She is a recipient of two NEA Translation Grants in the US and a PEN Translates award in the UK. She is the managing editor of Action Books. She resides in Ohio, where she is a professor of Spanish at Kenyon College, and Havana, Cuba. More information is available at www.katherinemhedeen.com.

Olivia Lott is a translator and literary scholar. Her book-length translations and co-translations include Soleida Ríos's *The Dirty Text* (2018), Lucía Estrada's *Katabasis* (2020), and Raúl Gómez Jattin's *Almost Obscene* (2022). Her translations have received recognition from the Academy of American Poets, PEN Literary Awards, and *Words Without Borders*. She is a postdoctoral research associate in the Program in Latin American Studies at Princeton University, and in 2024–25

she will begin as an assistant professor of Spanish at Yale University. Her scholarly writing has appeared in *PMLA*, *Revista Hispánica Moderna*, *Translation Studies*, and *Chasqui*. She is currently at work on a book manuscript on 1960s neo-avant-garde poetics and translation in Latin America.

WISCONSIN POETRY SERIES

Sean Bishop and Jesse Lee Kercheval, series editors
Ronald Wallace, founding series editor

How the End First Showed (B) • D. M. Aderibigbe

New Jersey (B) • Betsy Andrews

Salt (B) • Renée Ashley

(At) Wrist (B) • Tacey M. Atsitty

Horizon Note (B) • Robin Behn

About Crows (FP) • Craig Blais

Mrs. Dumpty (FP) • Chana Bloch

Shopping, or The End of Time (FP) • Emily Bludworth de Barrios

The Declarable Future (4L) • Jennifer Boyden

The Mouths of Grazing Things (B) • Jennifer Boyden

Help Is on the Way (4L) • John Brehm

No Day at the Beach • John Brehm

Sea of Faith (B) • John Brehm

Reunion (FP) • Fleda Brown

Brief Landing on the Earth's Surface (B) • Juanita Brunk

Ejo: Poems, Rwanda, 1991–1994 (FP) • Derick Burleson

Grace Engine • Joshua Burton

The Roof of the Whale Poems (T) • Juan Calzadilla, translated by
    Katherine M. Hedeen and Olivia Lott

Jagged with Love (B) • Susanna Childress

Almost Nothing to Be Scared Of (4L) • David Clewell

The Low End of Higher Things • David Clewell

Now We're Getting Somewhere (FP) • David Clewell

(B) = Winner of the Brittingham Prize in Poetry
(FP) = Winner of the Felix Pollak Prize in Poetry
(4L) = Winner of the Four Lakes Prize in Poetry
(T) = Winner of the Wisconsin Prize for Poetry in Translation

Taken Somehow by Surprise (4L) • David Clewell

Thunderhead • Emily Rose Cole

Borrowed Dress (FP) • Cathy Colman

Dear Terror, Dear Splendor • Melissa Crowe

Places/Everyone (B) • Jim Daniels

Show and Tell • Jim Daniels

Darkroom (B) • Jazzy Danziger

And Her Soul Out of Nothing (B) • Olena Kalytiak Davis

Afterlife (FP) • Michael Dhyne

My Favorite Tyrants (B) • Joanne Diaz

Midwhistle • Dante Di Stefano

Talking to Strangers (B) • Patricia Dobler

Alien Miss • Carlina Duan

The Golden Coin (4L) • Alan Feldman

Immortality (4L) • Alan Feldman

A Sail to Great Island (FP) • Alan Feldman

Psalms • Julia Fiedorczuk, translated by Bill Johnston

The Word We Used for It (B) • Max Garland

A Field Guide to the Heavens (B) • Frank X. Gaspar

The Royal Baker's Daughter (FP) • Barbara Goldberg

Fractures (FP) • Carlos Andrés Gómez

Gloss • Rebecca Hazelton

Funny (FP) • Jennifer Michael Hecht

Queen in Blue • Ambalila Hemsell

The Legend of Light (FP) • Bob Hicok

Sweet Ruin (B) • Tony Hoagland

Partially Excited States (FP) • Charles Hood

Ripe (FP) • Roy Jacobstein

Last Seen (FP) • Jacqueline Jones LaMon

Perigee (B) • Diane Kerr